Praise for *The Moral Imperative of School Leadership*

Michael Fullan confronts us with a most provocative paradox: on the one hand he acknowledges that school leaders are overloaded and overwhelmed by the demands of their schools; on the other, he argues persuasively that for schools to flourish in our society principals must extend their energies and take their moral purpose BEYOND the schoolhouse to the larger district, and to the profession at large. By doing so Fullan dramatically extends the boundary and redefines what it means to be a community of learners and of leaders.

Roland S. Barth
Author and Educator

Michael Fullan has brought much needed clarity to the main issues and to the key role of school leadership in meaningful education reform. His insights and recommendations will inspire anyone interested in lasting improvement in education. It is a must read, not just for principals, but also for those involved in the formation of education policy at all levels.

Michael Benson
Executive Director
Ontario Principals' Council
Toronto, Canada

Fullan sifts through the melange of leadership theories to highlight the real essence of leading schools: moral purpose. And most of what we require of today's school leaders has little to do with moral purpose. His analysis of the four levels of moral purpose powerfully and rightfully suggests that significant difference and change occurs when leaders look and lead from "below the surface" of the obvious. This book will change the way you view school leadership and perhaps change you as well.

Theodore B. Creighton, Professor
Executive Director
National Council of Professors of Educational Administration

This is a must read for any school leader interested in making a difference. Fullan goes to the core of what it takes to transform our schools and, not surprisingly, principals are at the center of the transformation.

Vincent L. Ferrandino
Executive Director
National Association of Elementary School Principals

Fullan challenges all who work in education to rethink the critical role of the principal as school leader in the current era of accountability. With clarity and insight, he offers a series of strategies to reshape the culture and context of leadership in schools to create learning communities where both students and teachers can excel.

Paul D. Houston
Executive Director
American Association of School Administrators

Michael Fullan has put his finger on the major problem at every level of school leadership: We have lost our moral compass. While he provides no easy answers, Fullan helps the reader identify the important question that must be answered by every leader who truly cares about the future of our schools.

Elaine K. McEwan
Author and Educator
McEwan-Adkins Group

A powerful call for leaders at all levels of the educational and political systems to acknowledge the critical importance of the principalship and to address the moral imperative of revamping this increasingly ill-defined role. A strong and passionate plea for recasting the role of the principal toward transforming schools. Fullan undertakes his assignment with remarkable insight and dexterity. And he does so by richly illuminating the meaning of moral leadership in a way that will capture the hearts of the women and men who lead our schools and school districts.

Joseph F. Murphy
Author and Educator

Fullan shows how moral leadership can reinvent the principalship and bring about large-scale school improvement. This is a masterfully crafted and accessible book by North America's foremost expert on change.

Thomas J. Sergiovanni, Author
Lillian Radford Professor of Education
Trinity University (TX)

Once again, the writing of Michael Fullan is a tour de force for those who toil in the vineyards of the school principalship. In this latest book, Fullan brings into clear focus the critical role of school leaders to "change the context" within schools—stressing the need to elevate the moral purpose of schooling in an era of accountability for academic achievement. Fullan makes the critical point—and sets an insightful direction—as to the equally important case for public schools to promote the personal and social development of students. Therein lies Fullan's challenge to school principals. The Moral Imperative of School Leadership *is a must read for those who want to make a difference!*

Gerald N. Tirozzi
Executive Director
National Association of Secondary School Principals

Being an effective leader in today's schools requires far more than dedication and skill. Effective leadership must be driven from a deep moral purpose, such as a belief that all children can and deserve to achieve at high levels and that educators can and are responsible for ensuring children's success. Drawing from research on effective leaders in education and business, Fullan provides specific and sustained attention to school leadership that is driven by moral imperative and fortified by shared leadership. More important, the main point of the book, that not only individual but system changes are needed in order for the principals to become powerful forces for school and even school system reform, is critical.

Michelle D. Young
Executive Director
University Council for Educational Administration

Michael Fullan

THE Moral Imperative OF SCHOOL LEADERSHIP

A Joint Publication

ONTARIO
PRINCIPALS'
COUNCIL
Exemplary Leadership
in Public Education

CORWIN
PRESS

For information:

Corwin Press, Inc.
A Sage Publications Company
2455 Teller Road
Thousand Oaks, California 91320
www.corwinpress.com

Sage Publications Ltd.
6 Bonhill Street
London EC2A 4PU
United Kingdom

Sage Publications India Pvt. Ltd.
B-42, Panchsheel Enclave
Post Box 4109
New Delhi 110 017 India

Printed in the United States of America

Library of Congress Cataloging-in-Publication Data

Fullan, Michael.
The moral imperative of school leadership / Michael Fullan.
    p. cm.
Includes bibliographical references and index.
ISBN 0–7619–3872–9—ISBN 0–7619–3873–7 (pbk.)
    1. School principals-Professional ethics. 2. Educational leadership-Moral and ethical aspects. I. Title.
LB2831.9.F85 2003
371.2'012—dc21

                           2003000010

03   04   05   06   10   9   8   7   6   5   4   3   2

Acquisitions Editor:	Robert D. Clouse
Editorial Assistant:	Jingle Vea
Associate Editor:	Kristen L. Gibson
Production Editor:	Melanie Birdsall
Copy Editor:	Cheryl Duksta
Typesetter:	C&M Digitals (P) Ltd.
Proofreader:	Kristin Bergstad
Indexer:	Michael Ferreira
Cover Designer:	Tracy E. Miller
Production Artist:	Lisa Miller

Contents

107987

Foreword

To come upon *The Moral Imperative of School Leadership* should not surprise anyone who has followed Michael Fullan's work over the years. The concept has been implicit in most of his writing. Indeed, he has made direct reference to education as a moral undertaking. It follows, then, that school teaching and leadership are moral endeavors.

Before reading the manuscript and deciding whether to accept his invitation to write this foreword, I began to wonder how he had addressed the sticky issues embedded in the word *moral*. When our book, *The Moral Dimensions of Teaching,* was published in 1990, the question most asked of colleagues and me was, "Whose morals are you talking about?" A little conversation quickly revealed that our interrogators held varying assumptions. Some thought that we had taken a stand on drugs, alcohol, and extramarital sex. Others thought that we had written a book on religion. And there were those who commended us because, they assumed, we had ventured into the realm of the spiritual.

We had just come off two comprehensive studies of schooling and the education of educators in the United States. In both, we had gathered an enormous amount of the familiar kinds of quantitative data. But, in both, we also had done a lot of walking around and conversing with people in the settings we studied. In the first, I always spent a good deal of time with the principals. Although our conversations might have appeared to be casual, each addressed the same common ground. One of my questions always was, "What do you see to be the central purpose of your school?"

The answers were disturbingly similar. They commonly consisted of two components that I briefly summarize: "There is no agreement here on this issue," and, "Our job is to give the kids a good education." Subsequent analysis of the hard data on schools individually and collectively showed high and balanced parental expectations for the development of personal, social, vocational, and academic attributes in the education of their children. Other data refined these general purposes to specifics such as equity, fairness, care, and civil interpersonal relationships. The descriptive embracing word that comes to one's mind is that these are *moral* conditions. Interestingly, in the earlier school-based discussions, nobody referred to the moral imperatives embedded in *good* education.

In the second study, we followed up these findings with specific items in questionnaires and in questions deliberately asked in the 1,800 hours of interviews we conducted in the teacher-preparing settings. We found little attention being paid to the purposes of schooling in the education of educators. Future teachers entering in or finishing the concluding student teaching phase of their programs commonly tilted their answers toward providing good education for all students. In answer to the question of whether this included creating a school and classroom environment characterized by and devoted to the development of civil and ethical principles, they said that it was a good idea but they had not thought about it very much. Some vaguely remembered something of this sort having been embedded in an earlier course but could not recall anything specific.

Participants in both studies were uneasy about the word *moral*. No wonder that I was curious about how Michael Fullan had addressed it in a book that boldly announces, in its title, moral imperative embedded in school leadership. He might have gotten off the hook a bit by referring to "educational" rather than "school," since the former is a very general concept and the latter is to a considerable degree a political entity buffeted by a variety of moral persuasions.

Instead, he simply assumes moral responsibility for schools and the education of those in them to be part of educators' guiding credo. This implicit assumption consists of two parts that become increasingly explicit as one moves along in his manuscript. The first is that the people of a social and political democracy are held together in a *moral ecology* that transcends the different interests, economic stratifications, cultural origins, religions, ethnicities, and races it embraces. They sense it and celebrate it. Since, for many, this ecology is to a considerable degree an abstraction, it is fragile. The second part of his assumption is that education of deliberate moral intent provides apprenticeship in the understandings, dispositions, and behaviors required for democratic citizenry. Providing this apprenticeship is a major purpose of our schools.

Michael is well aware that the nature of this moral ecology, and the education required to sustain and strengthen it is and always will be a subject of debate. But this is not what his book is about. Many excellent treatises on these matters are available. Instead, he leads readers through a much broadened concept of the educational domains school leaders must encompass in seeking to fulfill the moral imperative.

There is also an interesting pedagogical assumption running through the book. Michael's inquiries into schooling undoubtedly made him well aware that the moral imperative of leadership in and for the schools of a democracy is little addressed in the preservice preparation of educators. But he also realizes that most of his book's readers are committed to lifelong careers and the continued learning such require. Wise man that he is, he knows that such people rise to high expectations when those they respect have confidence that they will.

John I. Goodlad
President, Institute for Educational Inquiry
Seattle, Washington

Preface

The 1990s was a dismal decade for the principalship. Expectations for schools piled up, policies became more prescriptive but lacked coherence, implementation strategies were neglected, leadership training and development were missing, and few noticed the looming exodus of principals through normal and early retirements. Above all, the principalship was becoming increasingly unattractive, even to, or one could say especially to, those who wanted to make a difference.

Under these changing conditions, the advice I gave in *What's Worth Fighting for in the Principalship* no longer seemed adequate (Fullan, 1997). *What's Worth Fighting For* was commissioned by the elementary school teachers' union (at that time, principals were members of the union). They asked me to write a book that would help principals cope more effectively in situations of multiple demands. Their charge was an odd one for an academic: They requested a book that (a) was deep in insights, (b) contained plenty of action guidelines, and (c) was concise. This started a style of writing that attempted simultaneously to get below the surface into the more powerful conceptions, while making the ideas accessible and actionable. The 10 guidelines for actions were:

1. Avoid if-only statements, externalizing the blame, and other forms of wishful thinking.

2. Start small, think big. Don't overplan or overmanage.

3. Focus on fundamentals: curriculum, instruction, assessment, and professional culture.

4. Practice fearlessness and other forms of risk taking.

5. Embrace diversity and resistance while empowering others.

6. Build a vision in relation to both goals and change processes.

7. Decide what you are *not* going to do.

8. Build allies.

9. Know when to be cautious.

10. Give up the search for the "silver bullet." (Fullan, 1997)

These ideas are still helpful but not up to the challenge of today's principalship. They were written to provide school leaders with a mind and action set that more or less assumed that on any given day the larger system may not know what it is doing. Perhaps this latter situation still prevails, but it is no longer acceptable or doable to expect great leaders to evolve in numbers in organizations that do not cultivate them.

It has become clear over the past decade that we need large-scale, sustainable reform and improvement. To achieve this, we must now work on the question, "What would the system look like if it did know what it is doing?" (Fullan, 2003; see also Fullan, 1993, 1999, 2001a, 2001b). I am talking about system transformation. This book is about how principals and other school leaders must become agents and beneficiaries of the processes of getting there. This represents a huge start-up problem because current strategies, even the seemingly most effective ones, as I later show, do not produce school leaders who are pivotal to system change.

Chapter 1 sets the stage by showing why changing the context is the main agenda. I make the case that if we don't focus directly on changing the conditions that surround us—the culture of the school, how one school relates to another, the school district's role, and so on—we will not be able to pursue moral purpose on any scale. I also contend that this goal may not be as insurmountable as it appears. Small changes in context can be leveraged to make breakthrough changes.

Chapter 2 identifies barriers to the current principalship that indicate that we have a long way to go, although the claim in later chapters is that we can make substantial progress by taking up certain policy directions.

The third chapter introduces the idea of four levels of moral purpose, going from the individual through the school and district to societal levels. Chapter 3 focuses on the first two levels by staying at the level of the individual school and community.

Chapter 4 encompasses the system as a whole, including the district and the state. The question still is what is the moral imperative of the principal in relation to these higher levels? The answer, in general, is that changes in the principalship are central to the task of transforming the system as a whole—that is, to generating and sustaining moral purpose across all schools.

The final chapter pursues the complexities of traveling the pathways of creating new roles for principals—one set focusing on what individuals can and should do; the other focusing on what changes are needed at the system level.

The net result is that the principal's role figures more prominently at both the school and the broader levels. My goal is to make the principalship more exciting and doable. It cannot require superwomen and supermen or moral martyrs because, if it does, we will never get the numbers necessary to make a system difference.

This book is about school leadership, with the principal or head of the school as the focal point. As I shall show, the principal with a moral imperative can help realize it only by developing leadership in others. It is the combined forces of shared leadership that makes a difference. School leadership is a collective enterprise.

The audience for this book is twofold: First, this book is for principals and all school leaders who want to make a bigger difference than they ever imagined they could; second, it is for leaders at all levels, including policymakers, who are in a position to alter the system, thereby creating conditions for transforming the principalship into a powerful force for reform.

I thank the Ontario Principals Council for their innovative leadership in promoting the principalship as a moral enterprise for the benefit of the public school system, for their openness to ideas and networks of learning around the world, and for their commissioning of and support for this book.

Robb Clouse of Corwin Press provided great support at every stage of production.

Claudia Cuttress, as always, thank you for producing the training materials that form the background of the book and for editing and producing the book itself.

A special thanks to the thousands of school leaders we work with in our management-of-change training across several countries: Canada, the United States, the United Kingdom, Australia, New Zealand, and several others. Much of what I have learned is embedded in our interaction.

And finally to my many coworkers, academic colleagues, policymakers, and practitioners: Leading and learning always go hand in hand. I have been blessed with working firsthand with great lead learners.

About the Author

Michael Fullan is the Dean of the Ontario Institute for Studies in Education of the University of Toronto. He is recognized as an international authority on educational reform. He is engaged in training in, consulting for, and evaluating change projects around the world. His ideas for managing change are used in many countries, and his books have been published in several languages. His *What's Worth Fighting For* trilogy (with Andy Hargreaves), *Change Forces* trilogy, *The New Meaning of Educational Change,* and *Leading in a Culture of Change* are widely acclaimed. *Leading in a Culture of Change* was awarded the 2002 Book of the Year Award by the National Staff Development Council. His latest book is *Change Forces With a Vengeance,* completing the *Change Forces* trilogy.

To the resurgence of school leadership:
This time let's get it right.

CHAPTER ONE

Changing the Context

Context, n. structure, framework, environment, situation, circumstance, ambience, surrounding

—Urdang (1992, p. 26)

Everyone would agree that the context is changing; few define reform as changing the context for the better. The leader's job is to help change context—to introduce new elements into the situation that are bound to influence behavior for the better.

How important is context? The recent Organization for Economic Cooperation and Development (OECD; 2000) PISA study (Programme for International Student Assessment) of literacy performance of 265,000 fifteen-year-olds in 32 countries puts it dramatically:

> PISA shows . . . that two students with the same family characteristics going to different schools—one with higher and one with lower socio-economic profile—could expect to be further apart in reading literacy than two students from different backgrounds going to the same school. (p. 21)

We can't easily change the socioeconomic profile of the school, but the basic point is made—change the context, and you change behavior. Context is equally—if not more—important than the background or personalities that people bring to the situation. This is Malcolm Gladwell's (2000) argument: "The power of context is an environmental argument. It says that behavior is a function of social context" (p. 150).

Part of Gladwell's *Tipping Point,* which is easy to miss and is incredibly encouraging for our purposes, is that it is not the heroic actions of tackling complex societal problems that count; instead, "*the power of context says that what really matters is little things* [italics added]" (p. 150). As he puts it, most of us will be "better [people] on a clean street or in a clean subway than in one littered with trash and graffiti" (p. 168). Most of us, to use another example, will pay attention to the plight of individual students if those around us are doing so.

The starting point, then, for changing context is not the external environment (although I get to that later); rather, it is our immediate situation. Change the situation and you have a chance to change people's behavior in the short run as well as beyond. If you want to change people's beliefs and behavior, says Gladwell (2000), "you need to create a community around them, where these new beliefs could be practical, expressed and nurtured" (p. 173). Selecting and supporting good leaders is a crucial starting point for beginning to change the context in powerful, new ways. The leader's job description, then, is to help change immediate context.

The power of context is usually seen as a forceful constraint— as a given that you cannot do much about. What Gladwell (2000) is saying is don't believe it and don't get overwhelmed by big environmental factors.

The key to change is new experiences. As Kotter and Cohen (2002) say, "people rarely change through a rational process of analyze-think-change" (p. 11). They are much more likely to change in a see-feel-change sequence. In this argument, the role of the leader is to work through a process that does the following:

1. Helps people see [new possibilities and situations]

2. Seeing something new hits the emotions

3. Emotionally charged ideas change behavior or reinforce changed behavior (p. 11)

Context is social, not individual. When you look closely at the major strategies for reform these days, you discover that they have individualistic assumptions: what students should know and be able to do and what teachers and administrators should know and be able to do. These are important, but in themselves they will not change situations and systems. You can have the goal of having a credentialed teacher in every classroom, but the effect will be blunted if you do not also focus on changing the culture and working conditions of schools. More important, if you do not focus on the latter, good teachers will not stay long—or come in the first place.

THE PUBLIC SCHOOLS WE NEED

My colleagues and I are conducting a policy audit in Ontario, sponsored by the Atkinson Foundation and the Gordon Foundation (Leithwood, Fullan, & Watson, 2003). Our purpose is to examine the present state of the public school system in Ontario and to identify policy options that will significantly improve the performance of schools and the system as a whole.

You don't have to go very far into the question of the role of public schools in a democracy before discovering that moral purpose is at the heart of the matter. The best case for public education has always been that it is a common good. Everyone, ultimately, has a stake in the caliber of schools, and education is everyone's business. The quality of the public education system relates directly to the quality of life that people enjoy (whether as parents, employers, or citizens), with a strong public education system as the cornerstone of a civil, prosperous, and democratic society.

As the main institution for fostering social cohesion in an increasingly diverse society, publicly funded schools must serve all children, not simply those with the loudest or most powerful advocates. This means addressing the cognitive and social needs of all children, with an emphasis on including those who may not have been well served in the past. For instance, a focus on academic achievement, such as improving literacy and mathematics, must include a commitment to narrowing the gap between high- and low-achieving children—addressing what in England has been termed "the long tail of under-achievement." In addition, public schools, especially in diverse multicultural societies, must include citizenship and what some people call character education. As Goodlad (2002, p. 22) observes, there is a low correlation between test scores and honesty, civility, and civic responsibility. He elaborates:

> The trouble is that the school reform enterprise has been prescribing the wrong medicines for quite some time. It has ignored the broad purposes of schooling in a democratic society, ignored the huge body of research that would be eagerly examined if the field of interest were something other than schooling. (p. 19)

In other words, both academic achievement and personal and social development are core purposes of the public school system.

In England, Michael Barber (2001) points to the danger of a loss of trust in the public system:

> The public is impatient to see substantial evidence of progress on the ground. . . . The danger is that, as the economies of developed countries grow, more and more people will see private education for their children as a rational lifestyle option. They would become correspondingly less willing to pay taxes to fund public education, which, over time, would become—in the devastating phrase of the sociologist Richard Titmuss a generation ago—a poor service for poor people. (p. 1)

Barber goes on to describe how such a flight to private schooling would erode social cohesion and lead to ever-growing inequality from one generation to another. Only if public education delivers—and is seen to deliver—real quality can such a prospect be avoided.

Similarly, in Canada, Bricker and Greenspon (2001) observe that although the public's confidence in the educational system of the 1990s was shaken they "never abandoned the principles of the public system. . . . And as the decade closed, it became evident that the public continued to view schools as critical agents of social cohesion, the common glue that binds society together" (p. 149).

In short, a high-quality public school system is essential, not only for parents who send their children to these schools but also for the public good as a whole. The key point: Improving the overall system will not happen just by endorsing the vision of a strong public school system; principals in particular must be cognizant that changing their schools and the system is a simultaneous proposition.

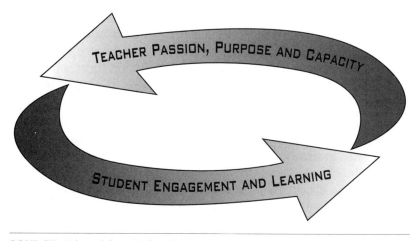

TEACHER PASSION, PURPOSE AND CAPACITY

STUDENT ENGAGEMENT AND LEARNING

SOURCE: Adapted from Fullan (2003)

THE PRINCIPALS AND TEACHERS WE NEED

In complex societies, producing and sustaining a vital public school system is a tall order. Let me state at the outset that you cannot do this without a dedicated, highly competent teaching force—teachers in numbers, working together for the continuous betterment of the schools. And you cannot get teachers working like this without leaders at all levels guiding and supporting the process. The principal's role is pivotal in this equation.

In *Change Forces With a Vengeance* (2003), I equated teacher passion, purpose, and capacity with student engagement and learning as in the following diagram:

Most people would place teacher commitment as causally prior to student engagement. In a technical sense this might be right, but emotionally the two are fused. If we don't think of producing teacher and student development simultaneously, we will miss the point.

In *Change Forces With a Vengeance* (2003), I reviewed several successful districts and the case of England, a country that significantly improved literacy and mathematics over a 4- to 5-year period. These strategies required great effort and coordination from top policymakers. I made a telling observation:

As the strategy unfolds leaders must pay close attention to whether they are generating passion, purpose and energy— intrinsic motivation—on the part of principals and teachers. Failure to gain on this problem is a sure-fire indicator that the strategy will fail sooner than later. (Fullan, 2003, pp. 62–63)

Michael Barber (2002), one of the principal policymakers in the British government, captured the dilemma in the evolution of the teaching profession in an insightful analysis in which he cross-tabulated two axes—knowledge-poor versus knowledge-rich strategies or conditions and national (or external) prescription versus professional judgment. The ensuing labels of the four quadrants are revealing of the past 30 or so years:

- Uninformed professional judgment (knowledge-poor/ professional judgment)
- Uninformed prescription (knowledge-poor/external prescription)
- Informed prescription (knowledge-rich/external prescription)
- Informed professional judgment (knowledge-rich/professional judgment)

These are fairly accurate generalizations. In the 1970s, when teachers had a great deal of autonomy (behind the classroom door) but not much disciplined deliberation (inside and outside the school) over what they were doing, the public had little idea about how well schools were performing nor was there any reason to believe that disciplined inquiry was guiding the day-to-day decisions of principals and teachers. Hargreaves (in press) prefers the term *permissive individualism* over *uniformed professional judgment*, arguing that there were many excellent teachers along with many who were not so good. The main point is the same: There was no system of collective deliberations focusing on continuous improvement.

In the 1980s, when accountability and standards were first introduced without much knowledge of how best to implement standards (knowledge-poor), leaders accomplished little other than alienating the better teachers with unhelpful intrusions. The first instances of accountability and many of the current versions are prescriptive but are missing key ingredients, such as capacity-building strategies. They are uninformed on the strategies and conditions for success and often incomplete when it comes to the purposes and goals of education itself.

In the 1990s, when some systems (still the minority) began using better knowledge and investing in capacity-building training of principals and teachers, there were some basic improvements, for example, in literacy and mathematics. But because these strategies were tightly orchestrated from the center, principal and teacher ownership—the kind of ownership that would be necessary to go deeper on a sustained basis—did not exist.

Finally, we arrive at informed professional judgment. There are two problems with this concept: What exactly is it and how do you get there if the starting point is low capacity? I won't answer these questions in detail, but any responses are pertinent to matters of moral purpose and context change. First, informed professional judgment is collective, not individualistic. It must be driven by best knowledge, which must be pursued continually through cultures of interaction inside and outside the school. It must have a solid moral purpose as a foundation. How you create conditions of establishing and supporting informed professional judgment raises a perplexing dilemma. It takes capacity to build capacity, so providing professional autonomy to groups of teachers who don't have the commitment and wherewithal to conduct their work with disciplined knowledge inquiry and moral purpose will do no more than squander resources. It is too easy for aspirations of informed professional judgment to fall short, so we should ask the following questions: What does ongoing informedness look like and how do we ensure its continual presence?

As we address these questions, we get a two-layered perspective on the role of leadership. The first layer reveals that the role of principals is to help create and sustain disciplined inquiry and action on the part of teachers. The second layer concerns what has to be done to help create and sustain in numbers school principals who are this good. In essence, this book is about this two-layered perspective.

We obtain further insight into the teachers and principals we need from Jim Collins's (2001) analysis of companies that go from good to great. Studying a sample of 1,435 companies that appeared in *Fortune 500* from 1965 to 1995, Collins and his research team

Level 5 Leadership	First Who Then What	Confront the Brutal Facts	Hedgehog Concept	Culture of Discipline	Technology Accelerates
Disciplined People		Disciplined Thought		Disciplined Action	

SOURCE: Collins, 2001, p. 12

became interested in companies that had sustained financial success over a minimum of 15 years. In the final analysis, only 11 companies qualified.

Collins's research is essentially a story of passion, focus, inquiry, and action—collectively pursued. Collins identified six core factors of success that he organized into the three themes of disciplined people, disciplined thought, and disciplined action:

Many of Collins's (2001) findings are central to questions of school leadership. Before presenting his ideas, there are two major limitations to his work that should be noted (I am indebted to Tom Sergiovanni for raising these issues; personal communication, January 2003). First, Collins relies on a single measure of success—financial performance. Second, his book is not about moral purpose: The 11 great organizations set out to be the best they possibly could be at what they were doing; there was nothing about moral purpose that characterized their work (for discussions of the role of moral purpose in business see Fullan, 2001b, and Hilton & Gibbons, 2002).

Be that as it may, Collins's findings about leadership are germane to our interest in what it would take to develop great schools. Put another way, think of Collins's core concepts in the service of the moral imperative. Collins summarizes his main findings as follows:

Level 5 Leadership

We were surprised, shocked really, to discover the type of leadership required for turning a good company into a great one. Compared to high-profile leaders with big personalities who make headlines and become celebrities, the good-to-great leaders seem to have come from Mars. Self-effacing, quiet, reserved, even shy—these leaders are a paradoxical blend of personal humility and professional will. They are more like Lincoln and Socrates than Patton or Caesar.

First Who . . . Then What. We expected that good-to-great leaders would begin setting a new vision and strategy. We found instead that they *first* got the right people on the bus, the wrong people off the bus, and the right people in the right seats—and *then* they figured out where to drive it. The old adage "People are your most important asset" turns out to be wrong. People are *not* your most important asset. The *right* people are.

Confront the Brutal Facts (Yet Never Lose Faith). We learned that a former prisoner of war had more to teach us about what it takes to find a path to greatness than most books on corporate strategy. Every good-to-great company embraced what we came to call the Stockdale Paradox: You must maintain unwavering faith that you can and will prevail in the end, regardless of the difficulties, AND *at the same time* have the discipline to confront the most brutal facts of your current reality, whatever they might be.

The Hedgehog Concept (Simplicity Within the Three Circles). To go from good to great requires transcending the curse of competence. Just because something is your core business—just because you've been doing it for years or perhaps even decades—does not necessarily mean you can be the best in the world at it. And if you cannot be the best in the world at your core business, then your core business absolutely cannot form the basis of a great company. It must be replaced with a simple concept that reflects deep understanding of three intersecting circles (what you are deeply passionate about; what you can be best at; what drives your economic engine).

A Culture of Discipline. All companies have a culture, some companies have discipline, but few companies have a *culture of discipline.* When you have disciplined people, you don't need hierarchy. When you have disciplined thought, you don't need bureaucracy. When you have disciplined action, you don't need excessive controls. When you combine a culture of discipline with an ethic of entrepreneurship, you get the magical alchemy of great performance.

Technology Accelerators. Good-to-great companies *think* differently about the role of technology. They never use technology as the primary means of igniting a transformation. Yet, paradoxically, they are pioneers in the application of *carefully selected* technology. We learned that technology by itself is never a primary, root case of either greatness or decline. (Collins, 2001, p. 12–14, italics in original)

Collins's five-level hierarchy is especially noteworthy:

Level 5: Executive

Builds enduring greatness through a paradoxical blend of personal humility and professional will.

Level 4: Effective Leader

Catalyzes commitment to and vigorous pursuit of a clear and compelling vision, stimulating higher performance standards

Level 3: Competent Manager

Organizes people and resources toward the effective and efficient pursuit of predetermined objectives

Level 2: Contributing Team Member

Contributes individual capabilities to the achievement of group objectives and works effectively with others in a group setting

Level 1: Highly Capable Individual

Makes productive contributions through talent, knowledge, skills, and good work habits (Collins, 2001, p. 20)

We can easily see the current principalship across Levels 1 through 3 and, in a small number of cases, Level 4. Such principals can be good leaders; they are just not great. And they do not help change the system. Even Level 4, the principal who turns around the failing school and obtains substantial gains in literacy and mathematics, is not building enduring greatness. He or she improves the context but does not change it. Changing the context means that what you leave behind at the end of your tenure is not so much bottom-line results (although that too is apparent) but rather leaders, at many levels, who can carry on and perhaps do even better than you did.

The principals we need are Level 5 leaders—more like chief operating officers than managers. The teachers we need are immersed in disciplined, informed professional inquiry and action that results in raising the bar and closing the gap by engaging all students in learning. There is no greater moral imperative than revamping the principal's role as part and parcel of changing the context within which teachers and students learn.

This is an exciting proposition and represents the moral imperative in its highest form. But, alas, we have very far to go and many barriers to cross. The next chapter delves more deeply into the current principalship—not all bad news and a necessary starting point for rebuilding the principalship.

CHAPTER TWO

Barriers to School Leadership

In September 2002, the Ottawa District School Board was one of three districts in Ontario taken over by the province for refusing to present a balanced budget. The province appointed a supervisor in each case whose job it was to find ways of balancing the budget. In the first week on the job, the supervisor saved money by appointing several principals to run two schools at a time, thereby reducing the number of principals in the district. What does this tell you about the image of the principalship? It is one of "managing schools"— Collins's (2001) Level 3 (at best) competent manager. We have our work cut out for us.

In writing *What's Worth Fighting for in the Principalship?* (1997), I began Chapter 1 with the following observation:

> Despite all the attention on the principal's leadership role in the 1980s, we appear to be losing ground, if we take as our measure of progress the declining presence of increasingly large numbers of highly effective, satisfied principals. (p. 1)

I went on to discuss a study of 137 principals and vice principals in the Toronto Board of Education in the 1980s (Edu-Con, 1984). Respondents were asked to rate 11 major expectations (e.g., new program demands, number of district priorities, number of initiatives from the Ministry of Education) as increasing, decreasing, or remaining the same in the previous 5 years. On average, 90% of the principals and vice principals reported an increase in demands, with only 9% citing a decrease.

In response to a direct question, no one reported a responsibility that had been removed. Some reduction was mentioned in teacher hiring, due to declining student enrollment. Time demands in dealing with parent and community groups (92%), trustee requests (91%), administration activities (88%), and board initiatives (69%) were listed as having increased, as might be expected. Parents, trustees, consultants, and teachers who were asked all confirmed that time and program demands on principals increased during the previous 5 years. There was one other finding about expectations and demands: Principals did not object to many of the new responsibilities per se, but in fact the majority saw value in many of the new programs. They were concerned more with the complexity and time demands involved in implementing the new procedures than they were with the procedures themselves. As I show later, the demands on the principalship are not the main problem; *the problem is the lack of opportunity for principals to shape the agenda and the limited resources at their disposal to make a difference.*

Principals and vice principals were also asked about their perceptions of effectiveness. Remarkably, even though the study used a self-report measure, 61% of the respondents reported a decrease in principal effectiveness (13% reported that effectiveness stayed the same, and 26% reported an increase). An identical percentage (61%) reported a decrease in "the effectiveness of assistance . . . from immediate superiors and from administration." The list goes on: 84% reported a decrease in the authority of the principal, 72% reported a decrease in trust in the leadership of the principal, and 76% reported a decrease in principal involvement in decision making at the system level. To the question, "Do you think the principal can effectively fulfill all the responsibilities assigned to him/her?" 91% responded "No."

Almost 20 years later, a similar survey was conducted in the Toronto District with 562 principal and vice principal respondents (Avalon Group, 2001). How much changed? A sampling of findings tells the story, though more negatively because the survey was conducted soon after a major amalgamation of several school districts in the greater Toronto area.

- Organization changes are effectively communicated:
  24% agreed or strongly agreed; 57% disagreed/rest were neutral.

- I am kept aware of significant developments in Board strategies:
  42% agreed; 37% disagreed.

- I believe that adequate training/support are available to help me improve my job-related knowledge and skill:
  45% agreed; 36% disagreed.

- I have the time available to access training opportunities:
  13% agreed; 81% disagreed.

- I feel the quality of my work suffers because of constantly changing priorities:
  63% agreed; 20% disagreed.

- I feel the quality of my work suffers because of lack of stability in the school system:
  76% agreed; 12% disagreed.

- I am able to recruit the teaching staff I require to meet the school's curriculum needs:
  33% agreed; 58% disagreed.

- The performance expected of me is realistic and attainable:
  30% agreed; 55% disagreed.

- I have a clear understanding of my role and responsibilities:
  68% agreed; 21% disagreed.

- The District has a clear understanding of my role and responsibilities:
  27% agreed; 57% disagreed.

- I am paid fairly for what I do:
  10% agreed; 84% disagreed.

- I believe the work I do is valued by the District:
  33% agreed; 48% disagreed.

- Time for coaching/mentoring staff:
  90% indicated not enough time.

- Planning teacher inservice:
  76% indicated not enough time.

- Delivering teacher inservice:
  79% indicated not enough time.

- Implementing curriculum:
  77% indicated not enough time.

- Completing paperwork:
  47% indicated too much paperwork.

- Level of stress in providing educational leadership:
  72% indicated it had recently increased; 12% reported a decrease.

The perceptions of the Toronto District administrators were no doubt adversely affected by the recent amalgamation of school boards and by the generally negative educational climate in Ontario, but allowing for additional negativity yields no interpretation that would allow us to discern any progress in the evolving role of the principalship over the past 20 years.

In fact, with the exception of a handful of districts in North America, the 1990s was a decade of neglect of school leadership. As problems of change became more complex, scant attention was paid to the development of leadership. That is now changing, as I concluded in *Change Forces With a Vengeance* (Fullan, 2003): Leadership is to the current decade what standards were to the 1990s for those interested in large-scale reform. Standards, even when well implemented, can take us only part way to successful large-scale reform. It is only leadership that can take us all the way.

As we contemplate and act on a new role for principals, what are the barriers we must overcome to move forward? They are considerable because they are deeply ingrained in the culture of the educational system. Even the most advanced forms of principalship, as I later show, fall short of the moral imperative.

For ease of presentation, the barriers to developing the principal's role can be divided into self-imposed and system-imposed categories. These are, of course, two sides of the same coin because they affect each other.

Table 2.1 contains a list of self- and system-imposed barriers on the development of the principalship.

Table 2.1   Self- and System-Imposed Barriers

Self-Imposed

- Perceived system limitations
- If-only dependency
- Loss of moral compass
- Inability to take charge of one's own learning
- Responsibility virus

System-Imposed

- Centralization/decentralization whipsaw
- Role overload and role ambiguity
- Limited investment in leadership development
- Neglect of leadership succession
- Absence of a system change strategy
- Limited advanced definitions of the principal's role, resulting in failure to realize the moral imperative of schooling

SELF-IMPOSED BARRIERS

Perceived System Limitations

Sarason (1982) suggests that principals may be perceiving more limitations in their role than is warranted. He begins with the observation that being a classroom teacher by itself is not very good preparation for becoming an effective principal. In their interaction with principals, says Sarason, teachers (as future principals) obtain only a very narrow slice of what it means to be a principal. This narrowness of experience is all the more constrained when the teacher's experience is limited to one or two schools.

Next, the newly appointed vice principal or principal often experiences emphasis on maintenance and stability from his or her teachers. Despite viewing their role as implying leadership, principals often respond in one of two ways when resistance to recommendations or ideas for change is encountered. According to Sarason (1982), they "assert authority or withdraw from the fray" (p. 160). This is, no doubt, an oversimplification, but Sarason's overall conclusion is that the narrowness of preparation and the demands for maintaining or restoring stability encourage principals to play it safe.

Sarason (1982) also claims that many people attribute more constraints to the system than is objectively warranted. These self-imposed conceptions of the system overgovern what they do:

> While I do not in any way question that characteristics of the system can have interfering effects on an individual's performance ... "the system" is frequently conceived by the individual in a way that obscures, many times unwittingly, the range of possibilities available to him or her. Too frequently the individual's conception of the system serves as a basis for inaction and rigidity, or as a convenient target onto which one can direct blame for most anything. The principal illustrates this point as well or better than anyone else in the school system. (p. 164)

Sarason (1982) then gives several examples of principals who were using atypical procedures in a school system, while other principals in the same system claimed that the system would not allow it, that it was counter to policy, that one would be asking for trouble if one took those actions, and so on. Sarason suggests that the tendency for principals to anticipate trouble from the system is one of the most frequent and major obstacles to trying new procedures. Sarason makes three important observations in his analysis:

> First, the knowledge on the part of the principal that what he or she wants to do may and will encounter frustrating obstacles frequently serves as justification for staying near the lower limits of the scope of the role. Second, the principal's actual knowledge of the characteristics of the system is frequently incomplete and faulty to the degree that his or her conception or picture of what the system will permit or tolerate leads the principal to a passive rather than an active role. Third, and perhaps most important, the range in practices among principals within the same system is sufficiently great as to suggest that the system permits and tolerates passivity and activity, conformity and boldness, dullness and excitement, incompetency and competency. (p. 171)

This, of course, is not the whole story. As we see in this chapter, there are many competing barriers conspiring to limit the effectiveness of the principal.

If-Only Dependency

Patterson, Purkey, and Parker (1986) talk about the nonrational world of complex society and identify a fatal flaw in our response to it, which they call the if-only problem. They observe that taking the position that "if only A and B would happen [one] could do [one's] job," "if only new teachers were better trained . . . , "if only the government would stop passing so many policies . . . ," and so on, inhibits forward movement. It is not that these observations are illegitimate complaints but rather that they assume that the system must get its act together before people can do their jobs. This is not a very good starting point for practicing principals because it stops them in their tracks.

Again, this is only part of the story, but principals must work at breaking the bonds of dependency, otherwise they will always be buffeted by the system. As I said in an earlier book, in the first instance, what's worth fighting for is more of an internal battle than an external one (Fullan, 1997). Paradoxically, transcending if-only thinking is one of the ways of changing the system that contains us because we take other actions that begin to change the immediate context in which we work.

Loss of One's Moral Compass

One of the great strengths one needs, especially in troubled times, is a strong sense of moral purpose. I discuss this in detail in the next chapter. In the meantime, I address how it is easy for principals to lose touch with the fundamental reasons for why they are in the role:

> When from our better selves we have too long
> been parted by the hurrying world, and droop,
> sick of its business, of its pleasures tired
> how gracious, how benign is solitude
>
> —(Wordsworth, *The Prelude,* cited in Storr,
> 1988, p. 202)

We saw earlier in this chapter that principals are constantly experiencing overload and a proliferation of expectations. This is a system problem, to be sure, but it is far more damaging if principals lose track of their moral compass. Why did I become an educator in the first place? What do I stand for as a leader? What legacy do I want to leave? (Livsey & Palmer, 1999). These are all-powerful questions that should be continually revisited; otherwise the principal's role becomes overloaded with emptiness.

Not Taking Charge of One's Own Learning

Hesselbein (2002) identifies a number of personal barriers to effective leadership, ending with "not taking charge of one's own learning and development" (p. 39). Because all organizations need to be learning organizations to be effective, the principal has to be the lead learner. If principals do not go out of their way to learn more (inside and outside of the school), regardless of what the system is doing they cannot become a pressure point for positive change.

The Responsibility Virus

Roger Martin (2002) has identified what he calls the responsibility virus, which plagues how leaders try to solve problems. There are actually two aspects of the virus—overresponsibility and underresponsibility. As he observes:

> Humans have a natural tendency toward all-or-nothing thinking when it comes to leadership and responsibility, and our responses are dynamic and infectious.
>
> One person makes a quick assessment of the situation and tries to take charge. But the strong statement "I'm in charge . . ." almost always carries with it the unspoken ". . . and you're not." In most cases . . . the signal "I'm in charge and you're not" prompts the other party to send a corresponding signal: "Fine. I understand. You're in charge and I'm not." Those initial signals, both the heroic and the passive, begin a cascade of reactions that lead to eventual failure.
>
> The heroic party reacts to the first flinch of hesitation, the first sign of passivity, by trying to fill what he sees as a void. This causes the passive party to see himself as being further marginalized, which prompts a further retreat, until he has abdicated all responsibility. And so it goes. (p. 4)

Principals, because of their middle-level position, are especially vulnerable to both strains of the responsibility virus. Individual principals may take too much responsibility vis-à-vis teachers or too little responsibility in relation to district or state policy. Martin (2002) describes the consequences of either condition:

> The overresponsibility sequence starts with "assuming singular responsibility for success," results in followers opting out, requires harder and harder work on the part of the leader (working alone to solve the problem), and eventually leads to failure. (p. 24)
>   Underresponsibility starts with "assuming minimal responsibility for success," focuses on others' responsibility not one's own, leads to feelings of disempowerment and vulnerability and subsequent failure to solve the problem. (p. 25)

The principalship, as I show later in this chapter, has probably bred more underresponsibility than overresponsibility but in either case results in ineffective leadership at the very time we need a massive increase in school leadership. I return later to the question of finding the cure for the responsibility virus, but it remains as one of the most powerful self-imposed barriers to mobilizing people in numbers to work together in addressing complex problems.

SYSTEM-IMPOSED BARRIERS

Centralization/Decentralization

If you are in the education business long enough, you can get hit by the same pendulum more than once. When it comes to centralization/decentralization, principals have had to duck on more than one occasion.

Centralization errs on the side of overcontrol; decentralization leans toward chaos. We have known for decades that top-down change doesn't work (you can't mandate what matters). Governments keep focusing on centralized solutions, either because they don't see any alternative or because they are impatient for results (either for political or moral reasons). Decentralized solutions, such as site-based management, also fail because groups get preoccupied with governance or lack the capacity to succeed. Even when they are successful for short periods of time, it is impossible for local developments to sustain themselves without external support and pressure.

The system barrier is the failure to realize that the principal is vital to resolving the top-down/bottom-up dilemma. In fact, the principalship is the only role strategically placed to mediate the tensions of local and state forces in a way that gets problems solved. Thus, the solution is to acknowledge the extreme importance of the principalship, clarify the power and nature of the principal's role, and invest in developing the capacity of principals in numbers to act as chief operating officers—that is, to operate as the Level 5: Executive Leaders identified by Collins (2001).

Role Overload and Role Ambiguity

The surveys cited from the Toronto District at the beginning of this chapter are likely typical of the principalship across North America. Almost everywhere you go, you see more expectations being loaded on the principalship. This explosion of demands on leaders, argues Robert Evans (1996), "decreases school leaders' sense of efficiency, and heightens their feelings of isolation, insecurity, and inadequacy" (p. 156). Virtually all of the principals that Evans encountered "acknowledge that their professional lives have grown more complicated and less satisfying, leading many to question not just whether the job can be done, but also whether it is worth the personal cost" (p. 156).

When so many demands are placed on the principalship, it is not just the sheer amount of work that is the problem, but it is also the inconsistent and ambiguous messages. Take control, but follow central directives; make improvements, but run a smooth ship, and so on.

The discouragement felt by principals in attempting to cover all the bases is aptly described by Duke (1988) in interviews with principals who were considering quitting:

The conflict for me comes from going home every night acutely aware of what didn't get done and feeling after six years that I ought to have a better batting average than I have.

If you leave the principalship, think of all the "heart-work" you're going to miss. I fear I'm addicted to it and to the pace of the principalship—those 2,000 interactions a day. I get fidgety in meetings because they're too slow, and I'm not out there interacting with people.

The principalship is the kind of job where you're expected to be all things to all people. Early on, if you're successful, you have gotten feedback that you are able to be all things to all people. And then you feel an obligation to continue to do that which in your own mind you're not capable of doing. And that causes some guilt. (p. 310)

When it comes to the principalship we want it all:

Wanted: A miracle worker who can do more with less, pacify rival groups, endure chronic second-guessing, tolerate low levels of support, process large volumes of paper and work double shifts (75 nights a year). He or she will have carte blanche to innovate, but cannot spend much money, replace any personnel, or upset any constituency. (Evans, 1995)

Limited Investment in Leadership Development

The 1990s was a decade of neglect in terms of leadership development. We are paying for it now as people try to play catch-up in the face of massive demographic departures and the reluctance of good people to take the role of principal under current conditions. Tom Williams (2001) captures this crisis in his recent study of the principalship in Ontario, *Unrecognized Exodus, Unaccepted Accountability: The Looming Shortage of Principals and Vice-Principals in Ontario Public School Boards.*

Williams's (2001) survey found that more than 80% of current elementary and secondary school principals in Ontario will retire by 2009 (two thirds by 2006). He also reports that there are fewer candidates for each vacancy—a trend noted across North America. Respondents were asked to rate possible "dissatisfiers." The six highest ranked factors (either rated as having a high negative or negative impact on the attractiveness of the principalship by at least 75% of the respondents) were:

1. Adequacy of time to plan for mandated changes (92%)

2. Number of curriculum changes mandated (86%)

3. Adequacy of time to work with students (83%)

4. Amount of in-school staff support (79%)

5. Amount of time the job required (78%)

6. Resources to meet school needs (72%) (p. 15)

Williams notes that all groups (principal, vice principal, elementary, secondary, male, female, all ages) ranked the same factors as the greatest disincentives.

It should be clear that when I talk about leadership development, I am not talking just about the principalship. The pipeline of leadership is crucial. You cannot have highly effective principals unless there is distributive leadership throughout the school. Indeed, fostering leadership at many levels is one of the principal's main roles. Thus, although this book focuses on the principalship, part of any effective solution is the improvement of leadership opportunities for all teachers. School leadership is a team sport.

The system is in deep trouble. There is a huge need for new leaders, and at the same time there is a set of conditions that makes the job unattractive—conditions that are well known to anyone working in schools. There has been such a lack of attention to leadership development that there is difficulty in filling vacancies at all, let alone filling them with people who possess highly developed leadership qualities.

Neglect of Leadership Succession

The problem of leadership succession is closely related, although even in the era when there were plenty of candidates, leadership succession was also neglected. If you look at studies of leadership over the years, you will find many examples focusing on the qualities of effective leaders and case studies of start-ups and ongoing leadership but hardly any research on what happens after a leader leaves.

Those of us studying sustainability identify succession as a critical factor in the equation. It is not turnover of leadership per se that is the culprit; rather, it is whether there is any attention to continuity of direction. What happens is either mindless replacement of leaders or hiring of new, high-profile leaders who are expected to turn the ship around with a new solution, which is often 180 degrees from the previous solution. As I said earlier, leadership policies should be judged not on how a given leader affects the bottom line during his or her tenure but on how many effective leaders—who are committed to carrying on and going even deeper—the leader leaves behind.

Absence of a System Change Strategy

In *Change Forces With a Vengeance* (Fullan, 2003), I argued that context must become the direct focus of reform, not treated just as a set of constraints. We need, in other words, to begin focusing on changing the system. Generally, current system-level policies are deficient. Since the mid-1980s, state governments have been attempting to get large-scale reform underway—that is, reform that would affect all schools. In our current initiative, reported in *The Schools We Need,* my colleagues and I (Leithwood, Fullan, & Watson, 2003) identified four major problems with reform policies in Ontario reform:

- The sheer volume of new initiatives blunts the impact of each.
- Distracting or inconsequential policies, such as teacher testing, and structural changes are unconnected to student learning.
- Policies are poorly implemented.
- Gaps exist in policies (e.g., failure to establish early childhood program, teacher induction policies).

Our point is that you need comprehensive, high-yield policies that are known to affect student learning. Most systems have enacted accountability policies in the absence of conceptualizing and investing in policies that would increase the capacity of educators to perform in new ways. The system is crucial if we want large-scale, sustainable reform. Until state governments tackle the problem of improving the infrastructure in a way that integrates accountability and capacity building, and does it in a way that is comprehensive, we will not get the leadership we need at the school level. In Chapter 5, I take up this question by discussing the kinds of policies that will be required to support the new role of principals as pivotal to system reform.

Advanced Definitions of the
Principal's Role Are Too Limited

Even the most advanced examples of the new role of the principal fail to grasp what will be required for fundamental breakthroughs. If we go beyond the principal as competent manager to the principal as instructional leader, the role is still too narrowly defined. Fink and Resnick (2001) describe the principal's instructional role:

> The idea that principals should serve as instructional leaders, not just as generic managers, is widely subscribed to among educators. In practice, though, few principals act as genuine instructional leaders. Their days are filled with the activities of management: scheduling, reporting, handling relations with parents and the community, and dealing with the multiple crises and special situations that are inevitable in schools. Most principals spend relatively little time in classrooms and even less time analyzing instruction with teachers. They may arrange time for teachers' meetings and professional development, but they rarely provide intellectual leadership for growth in teaching skills. (p. 598)

Through their focused work on the role of the principal as instructional leader, Fink and Resnick (2001) describe how they go about fostering such leadership:

> The development program for principals that we have described here is aimed at creating a corps of very strong instructional leaders who share a common set of commitments to teaching and learning, along with a sense of belonging to an effective and demanding professional community. More than just a collection of effective professional development practices, the program embodies a core set of beliefs about the nature of school and district instructional leadership, the centrality of professional development in educational administration, and the ways in which accountability for results and professional support systems should interact. (p. 605)

The principal as instructional leader is a good idea, but only as far as it goes.

As important as it is to improve literacy and mathematics, this is not the ultimate goal. As I discussed in the last chapter, England brought about large-scale improvement in literacy and numeracy in 20,000 primary schools in the 1997–2002 period. School leaders played a key role in these impressive accomplishments, yet, in this same period, the morale of teachers and principals did not improve due to a number of complex factors: the overall pace of change, work overload, lack of ownership of the strategy, and so on.

These centrally directed reforms with strong knowledge bases (whether orchestrated from the state or district levels) Barber (2002) calls informed prescription. In the best cases, they raise the floor, but not much of the ceiling. They result in an increase in teacher knowledge and skills but do not get at the motivation, passion, and creativity of teachers, and hence they fail to go deeper, and eventually they run out of steam. They require good leadership more like Collins's (2001) Level 3: Competent Manager (organizes people and resources toward the effective and efficient pursuit of predetermined objectives).

Barber (2002) argues that we should move toward informed professional judgment. Even this label does not capture the moral imperative and enduring greatness image of schools to which we should aspire. But assuming that it is in the right direction, what are the barriers to moving from prescription to judgment?

First, many teachers and principals may have developed a fostered dependency from the prescription period, and when invited to engage in informed professional judgment, they may respond by saying, "Tell us what to do." Second, it takes capacity to build capacity; hence, teachers and principals who have not worked together this way before may not know what to do. They may be motivated to engage in informed professional judgment, but they may not have the concepts, skills, and knowledge necessary to do it effectively. And they may think they are engaging in informed professional development but are actually not going very deep (i.e., they may not know that they don't know). Third, it is easy for this direction to drift into professional judgment without adequately pressing for the informed component. Fourth, we need to pursue these new directions in a way that is transparently accountable to the public. Finally, we need to go deeper, much deeper, in transforming schools. So the notion of accountable, informed professional judgment is a complex one and only a new starting point.

All of this is to say two things: One is that new directions call for sophisticated leadership at the school level. The principal of the future must lead a complex learning organization by helping to establish new cultures in schools that have deep capacities to engage in continuous problem solving and improvement. Second, there is a missing ingredient. What lever is going to be powerful enough to usher in the new era? That lever involves a radical revisit to the moral purpose of public schools. Moral purpose writ large is much more comprehensive than we might have imagined. It is impossible to have moral purpose on a large scale unless we recast the role of the principal as chief operating officer in transforming schools and school systems and, hence, the moral imperative of school leadership.

CHAPTER THREE

The Moral Imperative at the School Level

Let's be explicit. The only goal worth talking about is transforming the current school system so that large-scale, sustainable, continuous reform becomes built in. Moral purpose of the highest order is having a system where all students learn, the gap between high and low performance becomes greatly reduced, and what people learn enables them to be successful citizens and workers in a morally based knowledge society. The role strategically placed to best accomplish this is the principalship—not the current one but the one envisaged in this book.

Figure 3.1 visualizes a hierarchy of that moral purpose. As we move up the four levels, the figure assumes that each level encompasses previous ones. For example, those making a contribution at Level 4, by definition, need to be involved in the work of the previous three levels if they are to be effective, and so on. It is also the case that there are degrees of depth, as shown in the figure. One can make a useful difference part way below the surface or make a significant difference at a much deeper level. For example, teaching a child to read is an important contribution, but inspiring him or her to be an enthusiastic, lifelong reader is another matter.

It should go without saying that the current system is not conducive to achieving the higher levels of the hierarchy. Indeed, this is the point. We need to visualize and then create the conditions under which these levels can flourish. In the meantime, and deeply ironic,

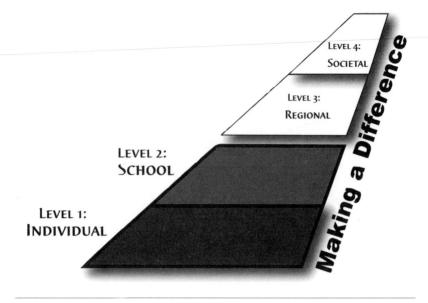

Figure 3.1   Levels of the Moral Imperative

those individuals most cut out for the higher levels are among those least likely to aspire to leadership roles in schools precisely because their highest moral purposes will be thwarted.

Before working through the four levels, I should also say that many aspects of the current principalship do not pertain to moral purpose at all. Being a competent manager, engaging in good public relations, and even getting higher test scores do not constitute moral purpose. What I am saying is that the driver should be moral purpose and that all other capacities (e.g., knowledge of the change process, building professional learning communities) should be in the service of moral purpose. In subsequent chapters, I take up the matter of the majority of principals—not just a heroic few—making this achievable, and I make my point that moral purpose doesn't mean being saintly. The new role of the principal must be feasible for all principals committed to making a difference.

In this chapter, I stay at the school level by taking up the question of what the moral imperative of principals is within their schools and communities.

LEVEL 1: MAKING A DIFFERENCE IN INDIVIDUALS

I won't spend much time on this level except to say that many principals are committed to making a positive difference in the lives of individual students and teachers. They may demonstrate this through personal attention and concern for individuals. They can help a few people, and this is no small contribution. But their impact can never amount to sustainable change because they are not attempting to change the way the school as an organization works. Recall that changing context is the key to deeper change, and to do that the principal with moral purpose must ask, "What is my role in making a difference in the school as a whole?"

LEVEL 2: MAKING A DIFFERENCE IN THE SCHOOL

Moral purpose becomes more prominent when we shift our focus to encompass the whole school. The criteria of moral purpose are the following: that all students and teachers benefit in terms of identified desirable goals, that the gap between high and low performers becomes less as the bar for all is raised, that ever-deeper educational goals are pursued, and that the culture of the school becomes so transformed that continuous improvement relative to the previous three components becomes built in.

Figure 3.1 displays different levels of depth with respect to school change. I use case study vignettes to illustrate the principal's role at different degrees of depth. Although not precise numerically, I present cases that I judge are at the surface, and at the 25% and 50% depth levels. This enables us to examine the principal's moral imperative with increasingly demanding criteria: In the course of presenting the cases, I draw heavily on Bryk and Schneider's (2002) significant study, *Trust in Schools,* because it focuses so directly on a core aspect of the moral imperative. I move through the cases inductively, summarizing at the end of the section the critical importance of Bryk and Schneider's findings.

Surface-level cases are those where what is being proposed sounds good and contains all the right concepts, where leaders can talk a good game and even mean it, but where the ideas never get implemented with consistency or integrity. A case in point is Bryk and Schneider's Ridgeway Elementary School in Chicago. The principal, Dr. Newman, articulates a strong philosophy of "students as his first priority," and staff as a close second. Bryk and Schneider elaborate:

> Dr. Newman knew that he needed to establish trusting relationships with all members of his school community to advance its improvement efforts. He was articulate about what this meant to him. "Trust is built by contact, by consistency, by doing what you say you're going to do, by showing concern, by acting on solutions, [but] mostly by doing what you say you're going to do." Throughout our interviews, Dr. Newman talked at length about the importance of positive social relations in the functioning of a good school, and felt strongly that developing trust was critical within his school community. (pp. 38–39)

Despite this attractive philosophy, Dr. Newman, in practice, attempted to be conciliatory with individuals and groups. Far from Collins's (2001) "disciplined thought and action" in "confronting the brutal facts" (p. 13) with respect to performance, the principal pushed a little but backed off in the face of any opposition. Conflict avoidance in the face of poor performance is an act of moral neglect. Bryk and Schneider (2002) make a number of observations:

- Relational trust atrophies when individuals perceive that others are not acting in ways that are consistent with their understandings of the other's role obligations. (p. 51)

- Although the principal appeared to listen to everyone's concerns, he rarely followed up on them. (p. 51)

- The stronger teachers at Ridgeway limited their interactions with other staff whom they regarded as behaving unprofessionally toward their students. (p. 51)

- Absent a base of collegial trust, a few individual teachers might attempt some innovations in their own classrooms, but larger initiatives that demanded coordinated effort would remain unsuccessful. (p. 52)

- Dr. Newman's seeming willingness to tolerate both incompetence and a lack of commitment within the faculty undermined his relational trust with parents, community leaders, and his own teachers. (p. 53)

Seems like a fairly straightforward case of lack of integrity and courage until you find out that many teachers didn't mind the laissez-faire approach—they preferred to be left alone. When it came time to renew the principal's contract (a responsibility of the school's Local School Council [LSC] in Chicago's relatively decentralized system), Bryk and Schneider (2002) stated the following:

> Many teachers attended the LSC meeting. . . . One teacher . . . voiced strong support for Dr. Newman. She spoke of Ridgeway as a "professional environment" and described Dr. Newman as a "very visible principal" who is compassionate and "caring" [and that] "it would be a big loss to the community if Dr. Newman does not remain at Ridgeway. (p. 43)

Two months later the LSC voted to renew Dr. Newman's contract "with a noticeable lack of enthusiasm" (p. 43). Surface indeed!

Another case, involving a principal with an even stronger vision, apparently undergirded by moral purpose, also ended up accomplishing little. The principal at Thomas Elementary School in Chicago is Dr. Gonzalez. On arriving at the school "he spoke passionately" (Bryk & Schneider, 2002, p. 56) about the ties between home and school:

> I would say that Chicago School Reform provides the opportunity for society to define a specific school that fits some kind of common values—a place that will be called the neighborhood school in which the values of the home and school are going to be similar. It is amazing to me how much discontinuity exists between the school values and the home values. Especially in the inner-city schools, you definitely find that there is a tremendous gap. For me, that is one of the basic reasons for school failure, the tremendous gap that exists between the school and parents. (p. 56)

Fundamental change was required at Thomas Elementary School. The principal attempted this by working with teachers as he fostered relations with the community. Again, on the surface it looked like a winning combination:

Strong principal leadership was needed to bring this faculty together. Dr. Gonzalez came to Thomas School as reform began. He articulated a vision for Thomas as a responsive institution to its local community. He sought to strengthen the role of parents in the education of their own children and demonstrated his personal regard for them through his day-to-day efforts at the school and around the neighborhood. He also recognized the importance of building a professional community among his teachers, and dedicated resources for their professional development (which was relatively uncommon in the early 1990s in Chicago). In many ways, Dr. Gonzalez offered a very appealing vision for both teachers and parents at Thomas School. Nonetheless, reform never really came together at Thomas during our three years of fieldwork there. (Bryk & Schneider, 2002, pp. 71–72)

As the principal pushed forward with reform, which included bilingualism (given a largely Hispanic clientele) and literacy improvement, he was unable to reconcile the conflict accompanying the changes with the trust and support essential for staying the course. As tensions rose, he "responded by taking a low-key approach" (p. 72). Once again we see vision-driven change that sounds good but fails to go far below the surface.

We can take a second set of cases, which I consider to be about 25% below the surface. This borrows from Level 3: Regional but provides a good illustration here for the principalship. The Baltimore City Public School System concentrated on improving the reading scores in 18 inner-city elementary schools that were among the lowest achieving schools in the District (Dicembre, 2002). Using a three-pronged strategy of adopting a quality balanced literacy program, intense professional development, and ongoing evaluation and feedback, reading scores improved substantially in 3 years. The principal's role, in detail, is not known, but a glimpse of it can be seen:

A key goal is to create instructional leaders so we provide professional development for administrators in both literacy and leadership. The leadership at each school . . . spend one day each month focused on literacy instruction. . . . In addition, principals and assistant principals have a full day of professional development each month focused on developing nine leadership competencies the Central Administration has identified. (Dicembre, 2002, p. 34)

Don't get me wrong: This is moral purpose, and many children are benefiting. But it is not very deep, may not last, and does not go nearly far enough in conceptualizing the moral role of the principal. Perhaps two examples of greater depth will make the point clearly by contrast.

Closer to 50% depth, consider Baxter Elementary School in Chicago, discussed by Spillane et al. (2002) in their study of school leaders and accountability policy. Echoing what I and others have found, that assessment literacy is a powerful tool for school improvement, Spillane et al. report:

Test score data represent an important instructional tool under the school's current leadership. In the context of staff development and curricular meetings, principal and teacher leaders send teachers a consistent message about the role of test scores within the school's own instructional agenda: for our own sake, let's use it! In particular, by using disaggregated test score data as an ongoing reality check on school progress, Baxter's school leaders have responded to district accountability measures in ways that enable them to build support for ongoing curricular and instructional improvement efforts. Discussion of test score data has become a regular feature of management and grade-level meetings, helping guide discussion of curricular priorities. (p. 739)

The principal (Mr. P), in collaboration with other leaders, established a strong evidence-based approach to improvement. As Spillane et al. (2002) conclude:

We rarely think of school-level leaders as "data crunchers," but at a school like Baxter, where meetings typically begin with the question, "What information do we have on this problem?" Mr. P now finds himself in good company. In 1999–2000, staff members (including the assistant principal, the dean of students, literacy specialist, and grade-level teacher leaders) volunteered to develop the school's annual district-mandated improvement plan. The group decided early in the process that the data collected by external state monitors the previous year was insufficient. To address this problem, they designed their own survey and classroom teacher interview protocol, a protocol designed to collect comparable data across teachers on classroom practice and staff development needs. After months of work, this data was compiled, carefully analyzed for cross-grade and grade-level patterns, and then compiled into a 20-page report complete with bar graphs. Indeed, as an organizational community, the school could rival a modern day corporation in its complex layered decision-making structure and highly regulated systems for making sure every teacher has input and that the input is gathered and aggregated. Every grade is part of a cycle; every cycle has an operations and a curriculum chair, and these chairs in turn make up the membership of the school's leadership committee. It was the leadership committee that was responsible, among other things, for reviewing the report compiled by the school improvement planning team. As part of this process, the grade-level leaders who composed the team reviewed and discussed the report's findings at one of the school's weekly grade-level meetings to cross-check for accuracy and gather supplemental data. (pp. 742–743)

Assessment literacy of this kind, which constantly accesses and disaggregates student performance data and develops and monitors actions designed to raise the bar and close the gap, and in turn mobilizes all stakeholders to play a role in this venture, is moral purpose with greater force. This can only be done schoolwide when the principal leads the process (see Rolheiser, Fullan, & Edge, in press).

Deeper still on our schoolwide moral purpose scale is the leadership of Dr. Goldman at Holiday Elementary School in Chicago (Bryk & Schneider, 2002). Note the language in the following passages:

"I feel a moral responsibility to a child who is innocent and vulnerable in this society to try—at least in my little neck of the woods—to give them a good taste of America. And I certainly will . . ."

"That's what I look for in my teachers—crusaders. . . . They're people who have a passion for what they're doing . . ."

He believed that Holiday School teachers must have a moral commitment to *these* children and *their* community. They must also have the professional skill to tailor instruction to the needs of each child. (pp. 77–78, italics in original)

We have heard this before, but the principal with the commitment and capacity to make a difference actually does so. At the beginning of the reform process, Dr. Goldman realized he had inherited a number of teachers with little interest in changing their classroom practices. Again reflecting Collins's finding that disciplined people is one key (getting the wrong people off the bus and the right ones on it), Dr. Goldman worked on creating incentives to encourage faculty who did not embrace the standards to either retire or leave. This process was time-consuming and required great effort. The result, as Bryk and Schneider (2002) report was as follows: Although it took almost three years, Dr. Goldman eventually was able to replace most of these individuals with new teachers who quickly came to share his commitment to strengthening the Holiday School community. (p. 78)

Incidentally, to anticipate Levels 3 and 4, there are moral limits to getting the wrong people off the bus, if they board another public bus that permits them to stay. This is precisely why we have to make corresponding changes at the other levels.

Dr. Goldman proceeded to forge a faculty that collaborated in instructional changes, assessment, and student results and made connections toward and facilitated interaction with parents. Bryk and Schneider (2002) observed:

The end result as we concluded our fieldwork during the fourth year of reform was the formation of a cohesive school community organized around a genuine regard for children. . . . As we exited Holiday School, we felt optimistic about its enlarged capacity to undertake serious improvement work. A faculty community—willing to take risks and commit extra effort to improve—had formed. They trusted their principal and enjoyed widespread parental support. Thus, key organization conditions were now in place for this school to accelerate its improvement initiatives, and, especially, to take on the complex and often conflict-laden decision-making associated with broad-based instructional change. (pp. 81–88)

Certainly the vast majority of schools are not at what I have called the 50% or deeper level. There are, however, many individual schools that approximate it. Our own case studies in 19 schools in three districts in Canada—Edmonton Catholic School District, Toronto District School Board, and York Region District School Board—provide several good examples (Edge, Rolheiser, & Fullan, 2001, 2002; Mascall, Fullan, & Rolheiser, 2001).

To take one example, the principal at Black River Public School in York Region worked diligently for a 5-year period to build a collaborative culture among teachers—a culture that focused on instructional improvements and student achievement in literacy. The principal demonstrated many of the characteristics identified by Newmann and his colleagues (Newmann, King, & Youngs, 2000) in their study of school capacity. The principal focused on teacher development, teacher leadership, a professional learning community, program focus, and resource requisition in establishing a strong school culture that resulted in marked improvements in reading levels in a school with a highly transient community population.

Another example of 50% depth moral purpose in action involves Lawrence Heights Middle School in Toronto and its principal, Chris Spence. The Lawrence Heights area consists of mostly public housing. Eighty-seven percent of the students or their parents are immigrants from 31 countries, and 24 languages are spoken in the school. Drug dealers, stabbings, and shootings are not uncommon in the area. During a 3-year period, student performance in reading, writing, and mathematics went from near the bottom of the heap to above the provincial average (see Spence, 2002).

Chris Spence says, "My approach is simple: put together the best people, support them and give them every opportunity to do their best work" (p. 10).

His daily diary reads like a compendium of what he calls the good, the bad, and the ugly. Hope drives improvement, he states. By persisting, not getting discouraged, pouncing on daily problems, celebrating success, selecting and supporting staff, and drawing on external ideas, Spence helps move the school forward—two steps forward, one backward. He elaborates on his role (Spence, 2002):

My mission as a principal is to bring a vision of dynamic and collaborative leadership to the challenge of public education. The intent of this vision is to build and maintain strong relationships and to encourage commitment and loyalty through trust, growth through participation and responsibility through accountability. My primary function as the principal is to continually acquire, as well as continually teach those being guided, individually and collectively, the attitudes, beliefs, values, knowledge and skills that facilitate success and move students and staff to higher levels of performance. (p. 25)

As with all effective schools working under adverse conditions, problems have to be immediately addressed and used as opportunities to reinforce school values, as well as to help those directly involved:

It was sad to see two of our grade 7 female students being arrested today. They were both charged with assault for their part in an ugly fight. . . . This incident sent shockwaves through the school so we quickly met with all students through grade assemblies to debrief and revisit our code of behavior and our safe school plan. We continue to communicate the message that a safe school is a shared responsibility. (p. 103)

As I noted earlier from Collins's (2001) study of great organizations, effective leaders work continually on selecting the right people and then developing and supporting them:

Deciding to go into teaching must be a decision from the heart. It must come from a moral imperative to ensure the success of all children and from a commitment to social justice. To be an effective educator today requires far more dedication, talent and commitment than ever before. . . . Schools that work for children have visionary leaders and dedicated and talented teachers who apply the instructional practices that research and experience tell us make a difference. I always aspire to study, seek advice, send staff to workshops, bring in experts and mentors, consult with others and use any means to increase our staff capacity to make good decisions. All the while I try to continually step into the unknown and encourage staff to do likewise. The risks, however, are calculated to push the boundaries of what is known and commonly done without threatening long-term success. (Spence, 2002, p. 142)

There are problems here. Under current system conditions, how many Chris Spences and talented teachers are going to be attracted to and stay at schools like Lawrence Heights? Even when you get a small percentage of such extraordinary people, how likely are they to stay with a rapid turnover of leaders? Indeed, after 3 years as principal, Chris Spence was promoted to area superintendent. Granted, he can potentially help develop principals of many schools from that vantage point, but maybe not, depending on the overall policies and politics in the district and in the province.

To anticipate later chapters, what if we rewarded moral purpose by giving extra resources (i.e., discretionary money) to attract leaders to work in difficult schools. What could be more powerful then to marry moral purpose and additional means to act on it? Further, what if we leverage moral purpose by providing resources and opportunities for the Chris Spences and their teachers to network with and help other schools in similar circumstances? As it stands, deep moral purpose is contained and confined to a small number of isolated cases.

Other individual case studies of schools confirm the essential characteristics of high-performing, high-poverty schools, such as the five schools in Texas discussed in *Expecting Success* (Council of Chief School Officers, 2002). Specifically, the principals in these schools led the establishment of cultures that, in concert, encompassed nine improvement strategies:

- Setting high expectations for all students
- Sharing leadership and staying engaged
- Encouraging collaboration among faculty and staff
- Using assessment data to support student success
- Keeping the focus on students
- Addressing barriers to learning
- Reinforcing classroom learning at home by engaging families
- Employing systems for identifying interventions
- Defining special education as the path to success in the general education program (p. 8)

I now draw some conclusions about moral purpose at the school level. I do this first by indicating the limitations of where we are now. Second, I consider how very substantial and deep the moral imperative of the principalship is—one that calls for dramatically enhancing the role and importance of the principal.

THE EMERGING IMAGE OF THE
MORAL IMPERATIVE OF THE PRINCIPALSHIP

First, I recap my previous discussions:

1. We need very large numbers of new principals, and we have a dearth of takers.

2. It is likely that only a minority of school principals are working at even the 25% level of depth of moral purpose I referred to earlier—a depth that improves, for example, reading scores of students.

3. Even the best examples improve only literacy and mathematics—impressive accomplishments in some circumstances but only first steps given the whole curriculum of the elementary level.

4. Whatever success has occurred has been at the elementary level. There are no examples of high school reform in numbers, only the odd exceptional success.

5. Fundamentally, there is little recognition of the depth of change in the principal's role that will be required. Policymakers do not seem to realize that the principal as booster of achievement scores is a dangerously delimited conception of what the principal needs to do for schools to be a force in societal progress.

6. We need principals who develop leadership in others, thereby strengthening school leadership beyond themselves.

We are beginning to obtain a glimpse of the new moral imperative of school leadership. At the school level—discussed in this chapter—the moral imperative of the principal involves leading deep cultural change that mobilizes the passion and commitment of teachers, parents, and others to improve the learning of all students, including closing the achievement gap.

We get a sense of the depth of the transformation required by considering what it would take to dramatically increase relational trust in schools, where relationships historically tend to be distant or fractious (Bryk & Schneider, 2002). I get to Bryk and Schneider's conception of trust later, but first I note the relationship between trust and academic achievement. Bryk and Schneider selected the top 100 elementary schools in Chicago (based on gains in student achievement in the 1991–1996 period) and the bottom 100 schools. They then correlated academic productivity with levels of trust in the schools:

> Schools reporting strong positive trust levels in 1994 were three times more likely to be categorized eventually as improving in reading and mathematics than those with very weak trust reports. By 1997, schools with strong positive trust reports had a one in two chance of being in the improving group. In contrast, the likelihood of improving schools with very weak trust reports was only one in seven. Perhaps most telling of all, schools with weak trust reports in both 1994 and 1997 had virtually no chance of showing improvement in either reading or mathematics. (p. 111)

Bryk and Schneider (2002) conclude, "As a social resource for school improvement, relational trust facilitates the development of beliefs, values, organizational routines, and individual behaviors that instrumentally affect students' engagement and learning" (p. 115). They elaborate:

> First, relational trust reduces the sense of vulnerability that school professionals experience as they are asked to take on the new and uncertain tasks associated with reform. . . . Second, relational trust facilitates public problem solving within an organization. . . . This is important because critical aspects of instructional improvement (such as curriculum alignment across classrooms and maintaining internal accountability among professional staff that all students learn) requires joint problem solving among teachers. . . . Third, relational trust also undergirds the highly efficient system of social control found in the school-based professional community . . . the resultant organizational norms strongly order day-to-day work, yet teachers still sense considerable autonomy and mutual support for their individual efforts. . . . Fourth, relational trust creates a *moral resource* for school improvement. School reform is a

long-term process that demands sustained adult effort . . . the level of trust within an organization influences the development of strong personal attachments to the organization and beliefs in its mission. When school participants hold such commitments, they are more willing to give extra effort even when the work is hard. (pp. 116–117, italics added)

Bryk and Schneider (2002) provide collateral data that schools with high trust in 1994 were more likely in 1997 to evidence greater "orientation to innovation" (seeking new ideas), "outreach to parents," "professional community," and "commitment to the school community" (p. 118) as a whole—all features associated in the research literature with greater organizational learning and effectiveness.

The school principal, of course, was the key person in developing relational trust, both in demonstrating it herself or himself and in fostering a culture of trusted relationships. Bryk and Schneider (2002) identified four dimensions or criteria on which they based their measure of relational trust. The four were respect, competence, personal regard for others, and integrity. These traits characterized the day-to-day behavior of more effective principals, and they also came to characterize the culture of the school and the community with respect to teacher–principal relations, teacher/principal–parent relations, teacher–teacher relations, and how all these groups related to students.

These are not just traits of the principal. They become embedded in the culture of relationships across all participants. All four are critical: "A serious deficiency on any one criterion can be sufficient to undermine a discernment of trust for the overall relationship" (Bryk & Schneider, 2002, p. 23).

Relational trust with a strong press for moral purpose produces very tough cultures that work diligently inside and outside the school to get results. They have many of the features of the "great" organizations studied by Collins (2001), although recall that these organizations were not addressing moral purpose. I am talking about very strong cultures. Collins talks about "the culture of discipline which build[s] a culture of people who take disciplined action" (pp. 123–124):

The good-to-great companies built a consistent system with clear constraints, but they also gave people freedom and responsibility within the framework of that system. They hired self-disciplined people who didn't need to be managed, and then managed the system, not the people. (p. 125)

It is critical to distinguish between the leader as disciplinarian and the culture of discipline, which characterizes the norms and working relationships of organizational members. Effective discipline is "a culture, not a tyrant," says Collins (2001, p. 129).

Collins then reports on several cases in which there was very strong leadership and short-term results that were not sustained:

[These] cases illustrate a pattern in *every* unsustained comparison: a spectacular rise under a tyrannical disciplinarian, followed by an equally spectacular decline when the disciplinarian stepped away, leaving behind no enduring culture of discipline. (p. 133, italics in original)

Returning to the earlier discussion of informed professional judgment, I now conclude that relationship trust and a culture of discipline must be part and parcel of any developments along these lines. Once again we need morally purposeful school leaders who can lead the transformation of cultures.

The nature of leadership required is strongly reinforced by Gerstner's (2002) account of the historic turnaround of IBM. In 1993, IBM was on the watch list for extinction, losing $16 billion dollars. With Gerstner as CEO, the giant IBM turned itself around, and Gerstner concluded his tenure in 2002. Gerstner says his strategy coming in was "strategy analysis, and measurement" (p. 187). Gerstner goes on to discuss the contrary:

I came to see, in my time at IBM, that culture isn't just one aspect of the game—it *is* the game. In the end, an organization is nothing more than the collaborative capacity of its people to create value. (p. 182, italics in original)

Gerstner stresses that vision, strategy, marketing, and financial management can set you on the right path, but no organization will succeed over the long haul without a culture of commitment and disciplined capacity building.

The point of this chapter is that leading schools—as in any great organization—requires principals with the courage and capacity to build new cultures based on trusting relationships and a culture of disciplined inquiry and action. That school leaders with these characteristics are in short supply is the point. Leading schools through complex reform agendas requires new leadership that goes far beyond improving test scores. Admittedly, developing trust and discipline in an organization that doesn't have it is a huge challenge. But again, this is the point: There are cases where it has been done. We need to learn from these schools, focus on the right things, and create the conditions under which new leaders can develop and flourish.

Now that a better conception of the moral imperative of the school leadership has been established, I move beyond the school to consider the system and the larger context. The limitation of Collins's 11 great companies, IBM, Holiday Elementary School, and the like, is that they are small in number. They are only a few organizations out of hundreds of thousands. For the moral imperative of the public school system to mean anything, we need to consider how the vast majority of schools can become transformed. Interestingly, if the school principal doesn't extend his or her conception of moral purpose to this bigger picture, not only will the system not change, but also the conditions for sustained moral purpose at the individual school level will be absent. There are, in other words, bigger fish to fry—a topic to which I now turn.

CHAPTER FOUR

Making a Difference Beyond the School

Recall Dr. Goldman, one of our morally driven principals, who made a great difference for children in his school. As he said, "I feel a moral responsibility to a child . . . *at least in my little neck of the woods* (Bryk & Schneider, 2002, p. 77; italics added). Well, in this chapter, I claim that the moral imperative will never amount to much unless school leaders also take it on the road. Sticking to one's neck of the woods guarantees that the moral imperative will never exist in more than a very small percentage of schools.

The argument goes like this: The overall environment must improve for all schools to continually improve (changing the context is key). The environment cannot be improved only from the top. The top can provide a vision, policy incentives, mechanisms for interaction, coordination, and monitoring, but, to realize this vision, there must be lateral development—that is, people at one's own level giving and receiving help (in effect, building capacity and shared commitment) across schools. In this way the moral imperative becomes a palpable, collective endeavor. If these developments play themselves out regionally, let us say across the school district or cluster of districts, it is far more likely leaders will be cognizant of their responsibility and contribution to closing the performance gap beyond their own narrow bailiwick. The result will be an improvement in the system—the district or region in this case. In the same way that the school cannot develop if individual teachers do not identify with and participate in schoolwide actions, the district cannot be effective if school leaders do not identify with and participate in districtwide developments.

That the current system does not make it worthwhile for school leaders to spend their time this way is the main point of this book. System leaders, I argue, must realize that school leadership is the key not only to school improvement but also to system improvement. In so doing, they will come to redefine the role of the principal as more akin to chief operating officer of a larger enterprise—the Public School System.

Admittedly, because it is a chicken and egg problem, principals with moral purpose should not wait for the system to get its act together but should already be pushing in this direction (and as I later show, there are increasing opportunities to do so). Such principals must strengthen and enlarge their conception of moral purpose, which is strengthened by seeing it as a moral imperative and enlarged by making a commitment beyond one's own school. Basically this means that individual school principals must be almost as concerned about the success of other schools in their district as they are about their own. This is the only way that large numbers of schools and communities will be able to operate with moral purpose, literally, because system action continually reinforces this direction through capacity building and accountable monitoring, all focused on moral purpose. This is Level 3; Moral Leadership applied to making a difference regionally (see Figure 4.1).

We are talking about a crucial development necessary for system change. Let me provide two contrasting examples, one that has little chance of affecting the system and another that is very much targeted to changing the context.

In November 2002, as part of the Leave No Child Behind Act in the United States, the federal government stated that parents of children who are attending poorly performing schools that are not improving can send their children to other, better-performing schools "where practical." The intention of this policy is honorable, but it has no chance of changing the system and hardly any chance of working for more than a handful of individuals. Individual parents would have to show a lot of initiative and face bureaucratic hurdles with little guarantee of success. Only a few will be able to carry it off, and the entire scheme will not even dent the system.

By contrast, consider, Bristol, England—a multicultural city operating under very difficult economic and social circumstances.

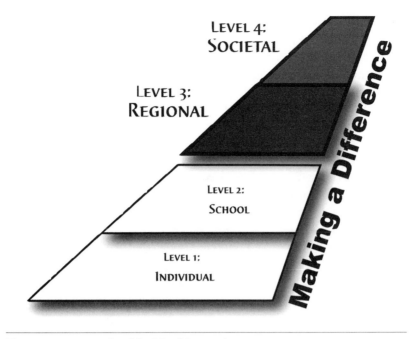

Figure 4.1   Levels of the Moral Imperative

There are 19 secondary schools in Bristol, 10 of which are classified as schools facing challenging circumstances (defined as schools falling short of the national performance target on certain measures). After some deliberation, a strategic plan was hatched by the 19 school heads and the Local Education Authority leadership. Each of the leaders at the 10 challenged schools will be linked with 1 or more of the leaders at the 9 more successful schools (school heads, department heads, etc.), and they will work together to improve all schools and the district as a whole. New Leadership Incentive Grants, along with local funds from the government, will be used to support this initiative. This is what I mean by a strategy that is designed to change the context. There is more to the Bristol plan than I have discussed, but the point is that the overall strategy mobilizes leadership at all levels to transform the system as a whole (Bristol City Council, 2002).

All of this is to stress that school leaders of the future must become increasingly aware of the bigger picture. What is the role of the public school in society? What are the key educational issues at the provincial and state levels? At the federal and national levels? I don't mean that principals should add saving society to their job description, but I do mean that they should be acutely aware of how the public education system is faring and how it is contributing to societal development, both in its own right and in comparison with other provinces, states, and countries. The more that principals identify with this bigger picture, the more that moral purpose will become a feature of the whole system, thus improving more public schools. In other words, identifying with and being concerned about the state of moral purpose in the bigger picture is a sign of great leadership. This is Level 4: Leadership—or making a difference in society.

We can now be more concrete about what it looks like to promote Levels 3 and 4 as envisaged in Figure 4.1. This represents a radically new direction for the educational system, so there are fewer specific examples. However, there are enough ideas to reveal what might be entailed and to bring us to the realization that there is tremendous untapped potential in pursuing these types of strategies and actions. The great hope is that such changes will change the context in powerful ways, thereby leading to system transformation.

LEVEL 3: MAKING A DIFFERENCE REGIONALLY

As policymakers and leading practitioners became more concerned that reform was confined to pockets of innovation, which are neither spread nor sustained, attention turned to going to scale. At a minimum, people began to say, "What does it take to achieve districtwide reform?" The majority of school districts do not have the conception, capacity, or continuity to be anything more than an episodic aggravation for school improvement (what Hess, 1999, p. 1, termed "spinning wheels and policy churn"), but since 1990 we have seen an increasing number of districts that can claim success, at least at the elementary school level (see Fullan, 2003, chapter 5 for a recent analysis of the district in large-scale reform).

In this book, I ask, "What is the role of school leadership in districtwide reform?" Once again I use the levels of depth in Figure 4.1 to explore this question because it is possible to have district reforms that appear to be successful but in reality only go just below the surface. Not being deep, the impact is limited. Moreover, shallow change, even though it may be in a positive direction, is less likely to be sustained. Put differently, deep change, which by definition involves changes in the culture, establishes conditions more likely to have staying power.

I consider several examples here. Most districts are still at the surface level or slightly beneath it. In other words, few districts have both raised expectations for principals and at the same time had principals interact and learn from each other.

As we go to the hypothetical 25% depth, let us return to Baltimore, a case in which reading scores improved in 3 years in 18 inner-city elementary schools using three policy levers: a new literacy program based on best practice, intense professional development, and ongoing monitoring (Dicembre, 2002). Not much is known about how school leaders learn from each other, but it is known that leaders spend 2 full days a month together. One day each month is devoted to professional development for school leaders, focusing on literacy instruction. On another day, principals and assistant principals are involved in professional development to enhance leadership competencies.

Moral purpose enters the picture because the mission of the 18 leaders is to improve reading in the most difficult schools in Baltimore. And they have. One can hypothesize that over the 3 years, spending at least 2 full days a month together, these school leaders learned from each other, built a sense of shared commitment for a difficult task, and had a great sense of collective pride in their accomplishments. However, we do not get a sense of the focus on culture or whether relational trust (among teachers, between teachers and the principal, and between the school and parents) substantially improved. We know from other research that schools can get results in test scores in 2 or 3 years by using intensive, relatively prescriptive strategies, without establishing a basis for going farther—indeed perhaps doing the opposite by burning people out (Fullan, 2003). The moral imperative, as I have argued, goes well beyond achievement scores.

A second example, and closer to the 50% criteria, is District 2 in New York City. With a strong focus on developing school leadership in its 24 elementary schools, District 2 moved from 10th place in reading and 4th in mathematics among the 32 community districts in New York in 1987 to 2nd in both by 1996 (Elmore & Burney,

1999). The evidence of culture change is captured in the seven ongoing themes or principles identified by Elmore and Burney:

- It is about instruction, and only instruction.
- Instructional change is a long, multistage process.
- Shared expertise is the driver of instructional change.
- Focus on systemwide improvement.
- Great ideas come from people working together.
- Set clear expectations, then decentralize.
- Establish collegiality, caring, and respect. (p. 266)

Fink and Resnick (2001) describe how the approach is based explicitly on principals learning from each other, as applied to the moral purpose of increasing student achievement:

Monthly principals' conferences are the primary vehicle for developing and building allegiance to the shared professional point of view of the district. Every principal in District 2 attends these day-long conferences (and usually a summer retreat of one or two days as well). The focus of the principals' conferences, without exception, is instruction and learning. Questions of administration and management are left to other occasions or relegated to a brief period at the end of the conference days. (p. 601)

How these strategies cultivate a culture of shared commitment across the district became evident when one of the schools in the district was put on the watch list because of low achievement scores. In most districts, the response from other principals would be to think, "There but for the grace of God go us." In District 2, because of the shared culture, other principals immediately contacted the principal in question and asked, "How can we help?"

My colleagues and I have been part of district success in systems that based their strategies and development on stimulating and coordinating school leadership. In the Toronto District School Board, the Early Years Literacy Project in 93 schools has resulted in improvements in a schoolwide focus in literacy, changes in instructional practice, and increased student learning with a focus on reducing the knowledge gap between high and low achievers (Rolheiser,

Fullan, & Edge, in press). School leadership—the principal and literacy coordinators as a team—played the key role in accomplishing these improvements.

As more districts engage in districtwide reform, my colleagues and I worry about the depth of changes and, in particular, whether school-based leadership is being strengthened in a way that will build relationship trust and other changes in school culture required for continually pursuing the moral imperative. Case examples include the recent studies of urban school districts that have been successful in improving student achievement across the district (Snipes, Doolittle, & Herlihy, 2002). My observations are not about whether the initiatives have been worthwhile. They certainly are examples of moral purpose in action. The case studies included Charlotte–Mecklenberg, Houston, and Sacramento, with the Chancellor's District in New York City as a partial case. Honorable mention was given to the Norfolk, Fort Worth, and Long Beach districts. The districts studied had all made greater progress in reading and mathematics than their counterparts and had all narrowed racially identifiable achievement gaps.

Interestingly, the case studies focused on district-level strategies, with not much mention of school leadership (although effective school-based leadership must certainly have been part of the success story, as I show later). For example, the lengthy executive summary's identification of the study barely mentions the principal (Snipes et al., 2002):

- They [the districts] focused on student achievement and specific achievement goals.

- They created concrete accountability systems . . . in order to hold district leadership and building-level staff personally responsible for producing results.

- They focused on the lowest-performing schools. Some districts provided additional resources and attempted to improve the stock of teachers and administrators at their lowest-performing schools.

- They adopted or developed districtwide curricular and instructional approaches.

- They supported the districtwide strategies at the central office through professional development and support for implementation.

- They drove reforms into the classroom by defining a role for the central office that entailed guiding, supporting, and improving instruction at the building level.

- They committed themselves to data-driven decision-making and instruction.

- They started their reforms at the elementary grade levels instead of trying to fix everything at once.

- They provided intensive instruction in reading and math to middle and high school students. (pp. xvii-xviii)

It is only inside the report that one gets a glimpse of the importance of the principal (Snipes et al., 2002):

- In all the districts, most of the focus on poor student performance came through principals. (p. 46)

- Sacramento and Charlotte-Mecklenburg made principals responsible for effective implementation of the curriculum. (p. 52)

- Houston . . . put on a five-day training institute to train lead teachers and principals. . . . District leaders also provided more extensive training to lead teachers, whom they hoped would guide the implementation of the curriculum. (p. 52)

In a summary table, Snipes et al. (2002, pp. 63–66) list preconditions (such as a shared vision at the district level and selling reform) and the nine educational strategies listed previously (focus on student achievement, accountability systems, etc.).

Within the case studies, references to the key role of principals are made, such as in the case of Sacramento (Snipes et al., 2002):

Strong school leadership is also considered a key part of the puzzle. Teachers credit their principals with giving them the support and training they need, trusting their professionalism, and building their commitment and support of principals. (p. 123)

What is my point? On the positive side, a picture of the critical role of the district in going to scale is becoming clearer. Without the districts, reform across many schools will not happen. Second, I am talking about effecting major moral accomplishments under adverse urban conditions, teaching many more students in poverty to become literate and numerate, and reducing the gap between high and low performers. This is a very important first step in raising the floor of achievement.

On the negative side, it is easy to lose sight of the emerging new role of the principal. Surely it is not to become a highly effective implementer of "informed external prescription," to use Barber's (2002, p. 3) phrase. To be clear, principals do have more resources in these districts, but they lie within fairly tight parameters. Second, and related, these strategies will not get us the cultural change and the relational trust identified by Bryk and Schneider (2002) that creates a "moral resource for school improvement," which in turn generates the passion and personal attachments necessary for "the extra effort" required to engage in the complex, long-term process to achieve deep reform (p. 117).

We get a strong sense of the limitations of a tightly orchestrated, external press for reform (even when supported with resources) when we see in every such case that these strategies inevitably take their toll on principals and teachers. They cannot be sustained. Snipes et al. (2002) describe the problem this way:

> Throughout the case study districts, principals and teachers reported that their jobs were much more demanding and stressful than in the past. Many reported that the continual pressures took a toll on their emotions and threatened to take the joy out of being educators and working with children. District leadership confronted this problem in several ways: by trying to improve the quality of facilities, materials, and administrative support that principals and teachers received; continuously stressing the importance of the mission of educating young people; telling those who did not want to increase their level of effort that it was time to leave; celebrating success along the way; and being visible in the schools and listening to what the staff had to say. Despite these efforts, the work remained grueling and everyone involved felt the pressure. (p. 62)

The moral imperative cannot be sustained on the backs of principals and teachers, who are driven by external forces even when the initiative does call on their moral purpose. Still, it is a start given the urgency of the problem. The question is, What is the next phase that can make moral purpose not only worthwhile but also energizing and doable? I address this matter in Chapter 5, although no one has the full answer, only promising directions and strategies (see also Fullan, 2003).

Earlier I discussed intradistrict involvement of school leaders. The same case applies to exchanges across districts for those school leaders who operate in consortia or clusters of districts. Especially in the United States, there are many states within which there are 500 or 600 districts that operate within subclusters of intermediate agencies. In other words, principals in multidistrict groups should be almost as concerned about the success of all schools within the consortia as they are about their own school.

Some of these arrangements are regional. For example, the Bay Area School Reform Collaborative (BASRC) was formed in 1995 to support school reform in the greater San Francisco area. Its core work involves 87 schools in five county districts, with an additional 1,465 schools in 40 districts participating (Bay Area School Reform Collaborative, 2002). The purpose of BASRC is to support school improvement through funding Leadership Schools, which are expected to bring about reform. They are also expected to promote and contribute to reform efforts across their member schools (i.e., across districts). BASRC has enjoyed considerable success in establishing inquiry-based reforms in its member schools. It has failed, however, in its aspirations to establish a regional learning community:

> BASRC intended to foster reform on a regional scale through Leadership Schools' examples and active efforts to foster inquiry-based change in other schools, crossover structures to build a regional reform community, and opportunities to share experiences. [However] . . . BASRC's Leadership School strategy to scale-up did not evolve as envisioned. While many Leadership Schools opened their doors to visitors and shared their experiences at collaborative meeting, most neither understood what it meant to "lead" nor had sufficient time, resources, or capacity to take a proactive role in leading other

schools' reform efforts. Nor were "followers" evident in large numbers. . . .

Crossover structures that BASRC constructed to foster a regional learning community—role-specific networks, collaborative assembly gatherings and critical friends, for example—nurtured an appetite for a regional resource and promise as a strategy to create a regional vision, but they had limited success in practice. Communication strategies within the collaborative were insufficiently developed and opportunities for BASRC participants to learn about the activities of Leadership Schools were limited. (Bay Area School Reform Collaborative, 2002, executive summary)

What this tells us is that (a) it is difficult for schools to learn from each other, (b) the culture and propensity to do so is missing, and (c) the resources and related capacity are limited. We would need, in other words, a much more explicit structure and a commitment from the formal system if we wanted to seriously move in this direction. Voluntary networks will not do the trick.

Recent developments in England provide a clear case in point with respect to promoting a deliberate strategy and expectation that schools must learn from each other if they are to have any hope of widespread reform. Minister of State for School Standards David Miliband outlines this strategy in two recent speeches:

If Government has an enabling role [in school improvement], our best schools need a leading role. To tackle underperformance, the best must lead the rest, whether in relation to the advance of transformational leadership, the spread of best practice, the modernization of the school workforce, or the development of partnerships with the wider community. (Miliband, 2002a, p. 1)

Miliband talks about the government strategy to invest in local development in exchange for a commitment to spread what is being learned. The government needs, he says, "to jump start improvement":

That is why for 1400 schools the Government will be investing £125,000 a year in each of the next three years, either to support existing leadership that is outstanding, or to improve leadership that is lacking.

The best heads will be encouraged to follow the example of Wigan, where three heads from successful schools are spending one day a week in a struggling school, Kingsdown High [with impressive results within 2 years]. (Miliband, 2002a, p. 5)

He goes on to emphasize:

> But networks of collaboration—local, regional or national learning communities—are also about culture and not just incentives. They are vital to a new culture of learning in the schooling system. That is why I celebrate the growth of networks of schools. . . . We want to see a schooling system growing from the bottom up rather than the top down, partnerships fuelled by vocation and interest and commitment, as well as contracts and funds, not central diktat. (p. 6)

In a second speech, Miliband (2002b) makes it explicit that he is talking about leveraging the moral imperative of school leadership within and beyond the walls of the school:

> Our starting point is . . . : school leadership is the single most important contributor to school performance. . . . If we accept that all our futures depend on the quality of education for all children, then we all have a vested interest in raising standards across the board, *not only in our own institutions.* (p. 5, italics added)

Miliband (2002b) acknowledges the difficulty in moving in this radically new direction:

> It is not easy to overcome a history of rivalry, resentment and suspicion. . . .
> For too long schools have been isolated. . . . Developing curricula, training teachers, stretching pupils has been done separately rather than together. Sometimes governments have made collaboration difficult. We want to make it easier. After all, education is about collaboration. The question now, isn't "whether," but "when," not about "who," but "how." (pp. 4–5)

Recall the previous example about Bristol—a clear case of school leaders banding together with district help and government resources to improve the system. This does represent a radical departure from the present order of things. It does involve going the full depth of reform envisaged in Figure 4.1. It would be easy to get it wrong. We are not talking about a band of noblesse oblige do-gooders roaming the streets and countryside blessing the downtrodden with their wisdom. Bryk and Schneider's (2002) four qualities of trust (respect, competence, personal regard for others, and integrity) come into play here, as does Collins's (2001) deep personal humility and "intense professional will."

This is hard, challenging work in which school leaders with a strong sense of moral purpose are expected to contribute what they know to others and supported in their efforts, in which those providing help learn as much as those receiving it, and ultimately in which all school leaders learn from each other. I am talking about a radical redefinition of the role and the importance of the principal, with corresponding capacity and resources to focus on improving student learning (raising the bar and closing the gap) in the principal's own school and beyond.

It should be clear that this is not just a matter of helping out a few schools. Rather, this is changing the whole system. If school leaders do not take their moral imperative on the road, system transformation will be impossible because you can't change the system from the center or from weakly supported grassroots networks. The new moral imperative implicates all school leaders in a shared mission to improve all schools

Level 4: School Leadership and Society

If school leaders were to do what we have just been discussing, they would save society, but that is not my point about principals and society—the fourth level in the moral imperative hierarchy. School leaders working with a strong sense of purpose and interacting with other school leaders regionally will enlarge the scope of their thinking in a way that benefits society. Societal development will be a by-product of deep implementation at the other three levels.

This fourth level takes us one step farther. The new school leader must be fully cognizant of the big picture. The most effective leaders are those who can see and appreciate the larger context within which they operate. This doesn't mean that school leaders must spend time at countless meetings or at the state, national, or provincial capital. It is more of a values and knowledge requirement. All school leaders should be aware of key state policies and should closely follow performance evidence on how well students are doing in the district, state or province, and country (in international comparisons). Student achievement studies should be of more than passing interest.

Effective school leaders must follow closely and be critical consumers of key developments in the bigger picture. This is not as difficult as it seems. Principals acting across the three previous levels will gain knowledge naturally on a daily basis. If other leaders in other schools are doing the same thing, they will teach each other— a seamless socialization of the moral imperative writ large. Principals as chief operating officers will come to know and influence the context within which they operate. In effect, this solution transcends the centralization-decentralization problem.

So, the little neck of the woods has become the whole forest— multiple forests, really. I cannot stress enough that principals cannot function effectively at the higher levels of the hierarchy without being deeply committed to the previous levels. When Heifetz and Linsky (2002) concluded that effective leaders have the capacity to be on the dance floor and the balcony simultaneously, they were talking about leaders with depth at all levels. The more a principal knows about one level, the more he or she will be able to influence other levels. Levels influence each other if there are strong developments occurring within the level (e.g., the school) and if there are norms and mechanisms that require cross-level (e.g., across schools and districts) interaction (see Fullan, 2003).

Is it possible for the moral imperative to operate on the scale I am talking about? Maybe, maybe not. But we do have an obligation to try, because school leaders working from a strong moral imperative foundation are the sine qua non of societal development.

The final chapter takes up the thorny question of how principals might start down this exciting new path in the evolution of school leadership. Ultimately, this is what's worth fighting for in the principalship.

CHAPTER FIVE

How to Get There

The Individual and the System

Peter Block (2002) wrote a book with the title *The Answer to How Is Yes.*

The answer could just as accurately have been *Why?* Block's point is that we too readily look to a how-to culture to obtain an external answer, thereby suppressing deeper deliberations of intention, purpose, and responsibility:

> My premise is that this culture, and we as members of it, have yielded too easily to what is doable and practical. . . . In the process we have sacrificed the pursuit of what is in our hearts. We find ourselves giving in to our doubts, and settling for what we know how to do, or can learn to do, instead of pursuing what matters most to us and living with the adventure and anxiety that this requires. (p. 1)

The first lesson of the moral imperative is, Don't forget the why question. Don't get lost in the how-to questions. For one thing, there is no clear answer to how to implement the moral imperative. There are orientations and guidelines, as I later show, but no definitive answer. The more we look for specificity at the how-to level, the more our self-reliance weakens and the more that intrinsically driven moral reform recedes. As we pursue the how-to-get-there question, we should always go back to first principles—the moral imperative writ large.

New directions and new contexts require both individual and system action, independently and, where feasible, conjointly. Individual initiative is required because we can't wait for the system to get its act together (or, more accurately, the system won't move in this direction unless pushed by individuals at all levels); system action is necessary because it creates new contexts, expectations, and support for individuals to change their ways.

THE INDIVIDUAL

I first revisit the nature of the journey so that those ready to embark on it know what it entails and how to relate to those around them. The most important thing to know is that the combination of moral purpose and relational trust generates the wherewithal to go the extra mile. It makes a complex, difficult journey worthwhile and doable. Bryk and Schneider (2002) explain why:

> Relational trust foments a moral imperative to take on the hard work of school improvement. Teachers had a full-time job prior to reform. Most worked hard at their teaching, doing the best they could for as many students as they could. In addition to taking risks with new classroom practices, reform also requires teachers to take on extra work: for example, engaging with colleagues in planning, implementing, and evaluating school improvement initiatives. Similarly, reform asks teachers to confront conflict, as this commonly occurs in organizational change processes. From a purely self-interested viewpoint, it would seem quite reasonable for teachers to ask, Why should we do this? A context characterized by high relational trust provides an answer. In the end, reform is simply the right thing to do. (p. 123)

What I am talking about are new cultures that are simultaneously supportive and pushy. Lesson six of *Change Forces: The Sequel* (Fullan, 1999) talked about this combination: "Collaborative Cultures Are Anxiety Provoking and Anxiety Containing" (p. 26).

The more we delve into the moral imperative in action, the more we realize that the ambience of anxiety is part and parcel of all movement forward. It is how we value it and contain it that counts. Heifetz and Linsky (2002) capture this tension in their recent book *Leadership on the Line: Staying Alive Through the Dangers of Leading:*

> Every day you must decide whether to put your contribution out there, or keep it to yourself to avoid upsetting anyone, and get through another day. You are right to be cautious. Prudence is a virtue. You disturb people when you take unpopular initiatives in your community, put provocative new ideas on the table in your organization, question the gap between colleagues' values and behavior, or ask friends and relatives to face up to tough realities. You risk people's ire and make yourself vulnerable. Exercising leadership can get you into a lot of trouble. (p. 2)
>
> Leadership is worth the risk because the goals extend beyond material gain or personal advancement. By making the lives of people around you better, leadership provides meaning in life. It creates purpose. (pp. 2–3)

Leadership, say Heifetz and Linsky (2002) is "about getting more out of life by putting more into it" and "putting yourself and your ideas on the line, responding effectively to the risks, and living to celebrate the meaning of your efforts" (p. 3). These days, doing nothing as a leader is a great risk, so you might as well take risks worth taking.

At the level of the individual, there are two major implications for school leaders. The first is to take action consistent with the moral journey we are talking about; second to push for and be responsible to system opportunities to deepen and extend moral purpose.

On the first matter, recall that leaders must establish a climate of relationship trust within which tough issues are tackled. Leaders have special responsibilities to initiate and lead new cycles of trust. Relationship trust is "forged in daily social exchanges—trust grows over time through exchanges where the expectations held for others are validated in action" (Bryk & Schneider, 2002, pp. 136–137). Principal leadership is central to these developments:

Given the asymmetry of power in urban school communities, the actions that principals take play a key role in developing and sustaining relationship trust. Principals establish both respect and personal regard when they acknowledge the vulnerabilities of others, actively listen to their concerns, and eschew arbitrary actions. If principals couple this with a compelling school vision, and if their behavior can be understood as advancing this vision, their integrity is affirmed. Then, assuming principals are competent in the management of day-to-day school affairs, an overall ethos conducive to trust is likely to emerge. (p. 137)

The tough side of the equation is equally critical: "Key here are principals' efforts to reshape the composition of their school faculties" (Bryk & Schneider, 2002, p. 137):

As principals seek to initiate change in their buildings, not everyone is necessarily affirmed, nor is everyone afforded a similar voice in shaping the vision of reform. Teachers who are unwilling to take on the hard work of change and align with colleagues around a common reform agenda must leave. Only when participants demonstrate their commitment to engage in such work and see others doing the same can a genuine professional community grounded in relational trust emerge. Principals must take the lead and extend themselves by reaching out to others. On occasion, principals may be called on to demonstrate trust in colleagues who may not fully reciprocate, at least initially. But they must also be prepared to use coercive power to reform a dysfunctional school community around professional norms. Interestingly, such authority may rarely need to be invoked thereafter once these new norms are firmly established. (p. 138)

These ideas are, of course, congruent with Jim Collins's (2001) conclusions about the good-to-great companies: Get the right people on board, confront the brutal facts, and establish a culture of discipline in which doing the right thing is built into the culture, combine deep personal humility with intense professional will—all difficult propositions in public schools, but this does not contradict their centrality.

These ideas are echoed by Anthony Alvarado, chancellor of instruction in San Diego City Schools District. I wrote elsewhere of the fragile nature of the reform in San Diego, in which district leadership has driven school reform in an assertive fashion (Fullan, 2003). In a recent interview, Alvarado reflects on the tensions in the process of reform (personal communication, November 2003). Recall that relational trust includes "competence" as well as "respect," "personal regard for others," and "integrity" (Bryk & Schneider, 2002). Every time principals focus on competence and better results under difficult circumstances, anxiety is endemic. Alvarado puts it this way: "Tension is part and parcel of the edge of success—learning to live with and work with tension is key to success" (personal communication, November 2003).

Collaboration is not an end in itself, says Alvarado, but a means of dealing productively with the tension. As he puts it:

> Having kids not educated in relation to race and class is a moral issue of enormous consequences. . . . [And] when we look at student work, for that work to be powerful, it needs to be tied to practice; when this happens it starts to become uncomfortable—then [because of the discomfort] the focus on practice weakens. It has to be tied to practice and results. Practice change is very hard for all of us. We must do the hard work of establishing in schools the kind of cultures that are prevalent in all great organizations. (personal communication, November 2003)

Alvarado adds that at this stage perhaps the impetus for performance is too much in the larger system and not deep enough in schools. Indeed, that is the point of this book—the need for trust-based practice and performance-oriented school cultures. Revamping the school principalship is key to greater performance on a large scale.

Staying at the individual level for the moment, developing a culture of relational trust and disciplined performance is very difficult. Such a culture must be guided, cultivated, and confronted. Leaders have to know when to let go as well as when to rein in. Reina and Reina (1999) provide further insight into this process in their discussion of transactional trust, which is "reciprocal" (got to give it to get it) and "created incrementally" (step by step; p. 64). They have identified three types of trust (reminiscent of Bryk & Schneider):

- Competence Trust (Trust of Capability)
- Contractual Trust (Trust of Character)
- Communications Trust (Trust of Disclosure) (p. 64)

As with all the research we have been reviewing, Reina and Reina do not assume that trust will evolve through mere invitation, good will, and expectation. All three components must be actively developed and reinforced by leaders. The subcomponents of each type of trust make this clear.

Competence Trust

- Respect people's knowledge, skills, and abilities
- Respect people's judgment
- Involve others and seek their input
- Help people learn skills

Contractual Trust

- Manage expectations
- Establish boundaries
- Delegate appropriately
- Encourage mutually serving intentions
- Honor agreements
- Be consistent

Communication Trust

- Share information
- Tell the truth
- Admit mistakes
- Give and receive constructive feedback
- Maintaining confidentiality
- Speak with good purpose (Reina & Reina, 1999, p. 82)

The biggest dilemma facing all leaders with moral purpose is what to do if you don't trust the competence and motivation of the people you are expected to lead. We have already provided one answer. Leaders need to take action to counsel out or otherwise rid the school of teachers who persistently neglect their own learning.

This is hard to do, but it is now being done in more cases. (The one caveat I mentioned earlier is that it does the system no good if such teachers join other schools.)

A second and subtler answer is the letting go–reining in balance. Leaders have a responsibility to invest in the development of organizational members, to take the chance that they will learn, and to create environments where people will take risks, tackle difficult problems, and be supported in this endeavor. In many ways, accountability or reining in is built into the culture: The day-to-day interaction among peers and between peers and others (e.g., students, parents, principal) creates a system of checks and balances, of learning and accountable performance.

Going down this pathway is very difficult to do, especially with leaders who have strong moral purpose. Failure to extend purpose and competence is the Achilles' heel of too-strong leaders. This is Martin's (2002) responsibility virus. In Chapter 2 I discussed Martin's important insight: Powerful leaders often assume too much responsibility for success (because they are impatient, because they see the answer to a problem). Such acts of overresponsibility cause other organizational members to back off, thereby assuming minimal responsibility themselves—a sure-fire recipe for failure.

Martin founded his analysis on Argyris's (1993) governing values. Martin (and Argyris) talk about the fear of failure, which is governed by four values:

1. To *win and not lose* in any interaction

2. To always *maintain control* of the situation in hand

3. To *avoid embarrassment* of any kind

4. To *stay rational* throughout (Martin, 2002, p. 34, italics in original)

This is all beginning to fit. Basic human tendency to avoid and attempt to eliminate or ignore anxiety is precisely what is not needed in situations of reform. Leaders, because they are in positions of authority and power, must role model new governing values based on relational trust and disciplined confrontation of problems. Leaders have a special responsibility to establish shared cultures or, if you like, new contexts:

Collaboration, by definition, occurs only when two or more individuals *share meaningful* responsibility for producing a choice. *Sharing* means allocating responsibility in rough proportion to each party's choice-making capacity. *Meaningful* implies that the act of sharing the load is important to the outcome: that is, one or the other collaborator could not accomplish the task on a consistent basis without the contribution of the other.

Without collaboration, as the complexity of a problem increases, there is no commensurate increase in the capabilities that can be readily applied to it. (Martin, 2002, pp. 66–67, italics in original)

Martin (2002, p. 103) provides a few "tools for inoculating against the virus." I must say that the conceptual and strategic ideas of the new cultures I have been talking about in this chapter are the most fundamental resources. Tools are only as effective as the mindset that guides their use. With this in mind, Martin's four tools can be very helpful:

1. The Choice Structuring Process

2. The Frame Experiment

3. The Responsibility Ladder

4. The Redefinition of Leadership and Followership (pp. v-vi)

A few words about each follow. The Choice Structuring Process provides seven steps for reframing a problem, with at least two solutions and brainstorming about their strengths and weaknesses.

The Frame Experiment aids leaders in changing the frame from the governing values ("I know the right answers; others are uninformed or ill-intentioned. How do I get others to see my way?") to an Altered Frame ("I may not see or understand everything others may see or know what others know. How do we access our collective intelligence?").

The Responsibility Ladder is a seven-step procedure for avoiding the breeding of over- or underresponsibility.

Redefining Leadership involves going from splitting responsibility unilaterally to doing so through dialogue, making apportionment discussable and subjecting performance and results to public (not private) testing (transparency of performance).

Martin (2002) has advice for those "mired in underresponsibility" (p. 181) and for those "trapped in overresponsibility" (p. 195). In summary, Martin's conclusions and advice are deeply congruent with what we have been talking about.

Thus he advocates going for:

- Informed choice versus win, don't lose
- Internal commitment versus maintain control
- Open testing versus avoid embarrassment
- Be authentic versus staying rational (Martin, 2002, p. 265*ff*)

The Responsibility Virus guarantees failure. Fear of failure generates more failure, and so on. Martin (2002) concludes:

> In embracing a new set of governing values, we choose to live our lives on the forward edge of our capabilities. This new way will produce failure, but it will be failure of a distinctly better sort. The Responsibility Virus produces hopeless failures resulting from extreme mismatches of capabilities and responsibilities, which leads to cover-up rather than learning. Failures under the new set of governing values—I predict—will be failures at the margin of our capabilities—failure from setting responsibilities marginally too high. From this failure we will be able to learn immensely, because our analysis and reflection won't be circumscribed by fear.
>
> With learning comes the enhancement of capabilities, not their decline. For each of us, the greatest level of self-actualization comes from building our capabilities steadily over time, but that requires submitting ourselves to a constant level of manageable stress. It also stems from coming to welcome, not resist, scrutiny of our performance by others. Stress guards against our under-responsibility and scrutiny discourages our potential over-responsibility. (pp. 268–269)

He also states, "Organizations populated with such people will run circles around organizations held in the grip of The Responsibility Virus" (p. 269).

All of this calls for new, radical forms of school leadership. Is this attainable for the average principal? It is not as far fetched as it sounds. I am not talking about high-profile, charismatic leadership. Indeed, such leadership is negatively associated with sustainable performance. Our most effective leaders are more solid. Badaracco (2002) talks about leading quietly. Quiet leaders display the following characteristics:

> [They] choose responsible, behind-the-scenes action over public heroism to resolve tough leadership challenges. These individuals don't fit the stereotype of the bold and gutsy leader, and they don't want to. What they want is to do the "right thing" for their organizations, their co-workers, and themselves— inconspicuously and without casualties. They do so by being baldly realistic about the complexities of their own motives and those of the dilemmas they face. (book cover)

In a series of case studies, Badaracco (2002) illustrates how quiet leaders resolve big problems by "a long series of small efforts [which] despite its slow pace, often turns out to be the quickest way to make an organization—and the world—a better place" (p. 2). Taking us through the swamp ("messy everyday challenges"), Badaracco makes the case that quiet leaders: "don't kid themselves"; "trust mixed motives" in themselves and others (self-interest and altruism run together); "buy a little time" in the face of complex challenges; "invest wisely" their political capital; "drill down" into complex problems; "bend the rules without breaking them" ("they do this after grappling with the complexities of a situation, not as a shortcut around them" (p. 126); "nudge, test and escalate gradually" ("Instead of a problem-solution paradigm, they rely on an act-learn-act-learn approach" and "craft a compromise by avoiding either/or thinking and looking for both/and outcomes)" (p. 128).

Badaracco (2002) refers to three quiet virtues: restraint, modesty, and tenacity. Heifetz and Linsky (2002, p. 226) identify three virtues of a "sacred heart"—innocence, curiosity, and capacity. And Collins's (2001) great leaders build greatness through a blend of personal humility and intense professional will.

My point is all leaders can move in this direction by becoming aware of the nature and importance of what is involved. All can take at least small steps toward these ends, gaining confidence and allies as they go. The leadership I am talking about involves strength through the middle not high-flying dominant saviors.

To be sure, the current system makes it much harder for school leaders to play these critical new roles. Still, because more systems are taking at least tentative steps in enlarging the scope of the moral imperative, it is incumbent on school leaders to respond to these initiatives and to push the envelope for altering district contexts.

Half of the responsibility, then, lies with individual school leaders. The other half, and one that must be taken up much more forcefully, is system action. The great irony in many systems is that individual teachers and principals have maintained their moral commitment despite the system. It is time that the system rewarded and enhanced those already working from moral premises and created the conditions under which all leaders will be expected and enabled to lead in powerful new ways.

THE SYSTEM

Despite what I have just said about the need for individual initiative, when it comes to the reality of large-scale, sustainable moral imperative, the system is a source of trouble. Current policies, structures, incentives, practices, and allocation of resources at the district and state levels can accomplish only 10% to 20% of what I am talking about. In other words, if we continue what we are doing, the moral imperative will never amount to much.

Here is a revealing illustration: Robert Stringer and his colleagues have been examining the relationship between leadership and organization climate for more than 30 years (Stringer, 2002). Stringer ended up identifying six major dimensions of climate (which resonate with most of the themes in this book):

1. Structure—Clarity and organization of roles

2. Standards—The feeling of pressure to improve performance

3. Responsibility—Feeling encouraged to solve problems on your own

4. Recognition—Feelings of being appreciated and rewarded for a job well done

5. Support—Feelings of trust and mutual support within the organization

6. Commitment—Sense of pride on belonging to the organization (p. 65)

When all six of these components are strong, in combination they produce powerful intrinsic motivation to go the extra mile. Stringer found that, of all the influences in organizational climate, leadership practices was the greatest. The 18 leadership practices Stringer identified are linked to the six dimensions of climate. The vast majority of Stringer's empirical work has been conducted in business organizations. Stringer (2002) did do one study in two high schools. The scores in the survey were standardized on a scale of 0–100%, as percentiles based on a larger database. The two high schools had remarkably similar profiles:

1. Structure—8% each

2. Standards—4% and 9%

3. Responsibility—56% and 67%

4. Recognition—4% and 5%

5. Support—10% and 11%

6. Commitment—10% and 13% (p. 169)

Scores this low, by definition, are rarely seen in the organizations studied by Stringer except in businesses with lousy climates and poor performance. Stringer (2002) comments:

I concluded that neither of the high schools has the kind of organizational climate associated with high levels of performance. The high levels of Responsibility show that teachers carry the high performance [when it occurs] in the two schools . . . the low scores in the other climate dimensions predict that it will be increasingly difficult to achieve high outcomes . . . I predict that low morale and teacher frustration will make it more difficult to introduce innovation and change to these schools. . . . Both high schools had been struggling with efforts to change for several years . . . the most important factors preventing the change are cynicism, disillusionment, and factionalism. (pp. 176–177)

Stringer concluded that the two principals did not do things that were directly bad for the climate; they were simply impervious to establishing a constructive organizational climate conducive to mobilizing the motivations necessary for high, continuous performance.

Of course, we could find better scores in some elementary schools, but not, I would say, remarkably high scores in most schools. In any case, the system question is not so much what leadership practices affect performance at the school level (we already know the answer to that question), but what there is about the larger system that produces so little of what we need.

The answer is that the system is not conducive to attracting, supporting, and developing the principalship we need for moral purpose to thrive. System transformation, of the kind we are talking about, will take at least 10 years (leadership is to large-scale sustainable reform in this decade what standards were to the 1990s; Fullan, 2003). At this stage, I can only outline some of the main policy and structural strategies that will most likely enable us to move substantially in this new direction (see Exhibit 5.1).

Exhibit 5.1   Strategic Directions for Transforming Leadership in School Systems

1. Reconceptualize the role of school leadership.
2. Recognize and work with the continuum of development.
3. Get school size right.
4. Invest in leaders developing leaders.
5. Improve the teaching profession
6. Improve the capacity of the infrastructure.

First, we need to reconceptualize the role of school leadership. The new role of the principal is closer in conception to that of the chief operating officer. The role is identical to Jim Collins's (2002) Level 5: Executive (builds enduring greatness)—except, as I noted earlier, Collins does not focus on the moral imperative—and to my four levels of the moral imperative. The change I am talking about means formally (in legislation and policy documents) redefining the role of the principal along these lines; devolving greater authority to the principal; providing more money and discretion over its expenditure; and, in the case of disadvantaged schools, allocating additional resources to principals to attract the best leaders. Strong moral purpose with the resources to act on its realization would be a powerful combination.

It should be clear that greater autonomy and flexibility do not mean isolation and loss of accountability. Just the opposite, as this book makes clear. The moral imperative writ large is a highly engaging enterprise both inside and outside the school. We must start by "visualizing the end result of the path we want to travel" (Martin, 2002, p. 198). The end result I envisage is principals who operate at all four levels of the moral imperative.

Second, we need to recognize the starting point and the continuum of development that will be needed. Most principals currently do not have the capacity to operate in this new mode. To expect great leadership in the absence of capacity is to squander an opportunity and resources. Some principals are not even on the continuum of school development. They are managers, at best running a good shop. We need, instead, organizational development, so our continuum starts with actions that are directed at schoolwide, instructional development. Andy Hargreaves (in press) frames this more targeted instructional continuum in an interesting way in comparing performance training sects with more fully developed professional learning communities. Performance training sects are based on strategies of what Barber (2002) calls informed prescription. Hargreaves contrasts the two forms in the following manner:

Performance Training Sects	**Professional Learning Communities**
Transfer knowledge	Transform knowledge
Imposed requirement	Shared inquiry
Results driven	Evidence informed
False certainty	Situated certainty
Standardized scripts	Local solutions
Deference to authority	Joint responsibility
Intensive training	Continuous learning
Sects of performance	Communities of practice

—(Hargreaves, in press)

In situations of low leader capacity, unprepared teachers, poor student performance, and a sense of moral urgency, it is sometimes necessary, as some urban districts have discovered, to start with the left column listed previously. This is okay, as long as principals don't get stuck there. The idea is to get the school on its feet and to address basic needs of literacy and numeracy but to do this in a way that paves the way toward the right column. Being aware of the long-term goal—that we are moving along a continuum and that we want greater decentralization—is key. The other five strategies in Exhibit 5.1 enable and support this development. Principals themselves must be part and parcel of considering the barriers and strategies required to keep the momentum going.

Third, get school size right. Bryk and Schneider (2002) observe:

> Relational trust among teachers is more likely in small elementary schools with student enrolments of 350 or less. This finding is consistent with basic organizational theory about the functioning of social networks. As organizations expand in size, subgroup structures form to coordinate the work. Concomitantly, informed social networks also arise, frequently based around common workgroup assignments. As a result, face-to-face interactions across the organization may become limited and these relations more bureaucratic. Individuals' primary affiliations are likely to be defined in terms of a workgroup or social network, and ties to the larger organization may be weak or nonexistent. Sustaining good communication across the organization can become difficult under such circumstances. Not surprisingly then, to sustain high levels of relationship trust is also harder. (p. 140)

High schools especially have to be downsized to 600 students or so. It is not only that school principals can more readily develop morally driven cultures in these small schools, but they also need to interact across schools. Managing a big factory-like high school makes interschool interaction and development impossible. In the meantime, don't wait for structural change to push for deeper moral purpose in all schools.

Investing in leaders developing leaders is one of the most exciting and high-yield strategic innovations of recent times. It is still at the early stage, so it has great untapped potential. We have always known that leaders' developing leaders within the organization is essential. As I said earlier, the success of a given leadership term is not just impact on the bottom line but on how many good leaders are left behind after the leader's tenure. We need to do much more of this intraorganizational leadership development. I have already discussed some ideas along these lines, including training leaders in avoiding the responsibility virus, evaluating leaders on their capacity to develop and nurture other leaders, avoiding appointing high-profile, charismatic leaders, and so on.

The new idea involves designing systems and providing resources so that leaders in one school can learn from leaders in other schools. I have already referred to some early, very promising models in Britain. After 6 years of informed prescription at the elementary level, England sees radical new school leadership as a "key lever for secondary reform" (p. 15) and for going deeper at the elementary level. England's strategy is based on investing in new leadership for all schools, and part of the strategy for moving in this direction is the following:

The best heads [principals] will be given new freedoms including:

- More resources on the front line (£50,000 more per school)
- More power to innovate to raise standards (earned autonomy)
- More power to deliver better teaching
- More power to tackle under-performing staff
- More power to form partnerships with outside bodies
- More power to expand and take over failing schools and to federate with other schools to share expertise, staff and facilities in new ways to raise standards

—(Department for Education and Skills,
2002, pp. 16–17)

One has to be careful about how this unfolds. Districts in North America have a greater authority-based role than do the Local Education Authorities in England. But the strategy is the same. We all should turn our attention to designing strongly supported strategies for developing many more leading school principals and for using them to lever more leaders inside and outside the schools as they go. Remember, I am not talking about superior leaders looking down on their less-fortunate counterparts. All through the discussions in this book, the best leaders have a multilevel moral imperative, personal humility, and intense professional will; they avoid the responsibility virus and see their role as systematically developing leadership in others so that sustainability can be achieved. Lead principals or heads with partial or full assignments to help develop leadership in other schools represent a powerful new strategy for transforming the system.

The fifth major strategy is improving the teaching profession. I have written elsewhere about the need to develop and combine two sets of policies: one that focuses on the individual development and performance of teachers and administrators and one that improves the working conditions of teachers (more time to work together, more support from paraprofessionals, etc.; Fullan, 2003). From a leadership perspective, these developments are crucial. As long as principals have hard-to-lead teachers (i.e., the current system does not breed competence and confidence in teachers), it won't be possible for principals to get on, let alone stay on, the course. We will get a few heroic stalwarts but never more than 10% to 20%, and they won't last. Put another way, we cannot get principals in numbers unless they are coming from and working with good teachers in numbers. The pool of quality teachers is an essential pipeline for the thriving principalship. We need better schools as places for teachers to work if we are to have better teachers and better leaders.

In addition to all the positive strategies one can put in place, included in the moral imperative is increasing "the capacity to remove incompetent teachers" (Bryk & Schneider, 2002):

We have already noted how the selection of new staff can promote alignment around a shared sense of obligations and thereby foster conditions conducive to trust formation. Of similar importance is the capacity to remove incompetent teachers from a school. We witnessed firsthand the corrosive effect that teacher incompetence had on the social relations of Ridgeway School. No one could really understand why some teachers were allowed to continue in their jobs when they refused to devote more than a minimal effort to their teaching, held very low expectations for children, and interacted with children and their families in demeaning ways. That such behavior was allowed to persist maligned the integrity of the whole institution. (p. 143)

Removing incompetent or chronically unmotivated teachers will not be easy—and it can be abused as a strategy to get rid of people who don't agree with you—but nothing undermines the motivation of hard-working teachers more than poor performance in other teachers being ignored over long periods of time. Not only do poor performing teachers negatively affect the students in their classes, but they also have a spillover effect by poisoning the overall climate of the school. System policy changes along with school leaders operating from a premise of the moral imperative can do something about this problem. And once leaders gain on the problem of reducing poor performance of some teachers, not only will good teachers appreciate it (tacitly at first), but also the organizational culture will become self-disciplined.

The final component for transforming the system involves strengthening the infrastructure for developing school leadership. You can't get large-scale, sustainable reform by devolving development. The infrastructure—the policies and programs at the local and state level aimed at developing leadership—is crucial. The direct question is, What is the capacity (e.g., at the district and state levels) to help lead and facilitate new leadership?

It is revealing to note that when Newmann and his colleagues (2000) studied school capacity, within which school leadership was a key factor, they hypothesized that programs and policies external to the school would be important in relation to fostering capacity. They did identify some schools with strong capacity, but they found no evidence that it was because the infrastructure was helping to produce it. It was as if having high capacity at the school level was the luck of the draw. You find it here and there, but there is no systemic reason to believe that it was deliberately developed or likely to last when it did occur. The new infrastructure must change this situation to one where a combination of forces works together to take us to new leadership levels.

The components of the infrastructure can be complicated in multilevel systems. I do mean state policy, which provides frameworks for what is expected and performance-based requirements for career-long development. I also mean policies that improve the working conditions of teachers and that introduce new resources for school leaders to lead other leaders of the kind described previously.

And I mean teacher union leaders who take the risk to insist on competence and capacity in their members as they seek greater public investment in the profession, all in the name of the moral imperative—leaders who embrace transparent accountability based on the strength of what the profession is actually contributing to the continuous improvement of all schools. Teacher leadership is part and parcel of school leadership.

The point is that leaders learning in context and fostering leaders at many levels is the core strategy of this decade. A coordinated major example of this new direction is Britain's National College for School Leadership (NCSL), which opened officially in October of 2002. NCSL is a state-of-the-art facility centered in Nottingham, England, and operating as an arm's-length agency with the purpose of promoting school leadership throughout the country. Its official aims are as follows:

- Provide a single national focus for school leadership development, research and innovation
- Be a driving force for world-class leadership in schools and the wider community
- Provide support for and be a major resource for school leaders
- Stimulate national and international debate on leadership issues (p. 3)

NCSL is responsible for overseeing and coordinating through local partnerships leadership development for all school heads in the country with respect to initial qualifications, induction, and continuous learning throughout the career of a school leader.

In other systems it may not be necessary to create a new entity. Existing principals' councils and school leadership institutes could play lead roles, as long as the initiative is systemic (i.e., coordinated so that whatever is done is integrated and systematic) and system driven (i.e., lead policymakers are valuing and guiding the effort).

As we observe school leadership becoming the force of the decade, it is essential that the whole enterprise be based on the moral imperative writ large—that the overall design and implementation encompass all six components (working in concert) in Exhibit 5.1. There is great action on these fronts in many countries, and it has enormous promise.

There is no more important journey for society over the next decade than the one on which the public school system has embarked. I have also made the case that we are not equipped for the challenges we will face in attempting to arrive at new destinations. The single key for unlocking the resources and capacities that we will need is an enlarged conception of the moral imperative of school leadership. Paradoxically, this amplified definition may make the job of school leader more attractive. It, of course, makes the work more meaningful and worthwhile for the leader. In addition, school development becomes more doable because the new leadership we are talking about mobilizes great effort on the part of others and attracts more resources from partners and from the public purse.

The moral imperative in the hands of school leaders with new mandates and more resources is our greatest hope for transforming school systems. It's time for school leadership to come of age. Prodigious accomplishments await!

References

Argyris, C. (1993). *On organizational learning.* London: Blackwell.

Avalon Group. (2001). *Survey analysis.* Toronto, Ontario, Canada: Author.

Badaracco, J. (2002). *Leading quietly.* Boston: Harvard Business School Press.

Barber, M. (2001, October). *Large-scale education reform in England.* Paper prepared for the School Development Conference, Tartu University, Tartu, Estonia.

Barber, M. (2002, April). *From good to great: Large-scale reform in England.* Paper presented at Futures of Education conference, Universität Zürich, Zürich, Switzerland.

Bay Area School Reform Collaborative. (2002). *Bay Area School Reform Collaborative: Phase one 1995–2001.* Stanford, CA: Author.

Block, P. (2002). *The answer to how is yes.* San Francisco: Berrett-Koehler.

Bricker, D., & Greenspon, E. (2001). *Searching for certainty.* Toronto, Ontario, Canada: Doubleday.

Bristol City Council. (2002). *Transforming secondary education in Bristol: A strategy for improvement of schools facing challenging circumstances.* Bristol, England: Author.

Bryk, A., & Schneider, B. (2002). *Trust in schools.* New York: Russell Sage.

Collins, J. (2001). *Good to great.* New York: HarperCollins.

Council of Chief School Officers. (2002). *Expecting success: A study of five high performing, high poverty schools.* Washington, DC: Author.

Department for Education and Skills. (2002). *Education and skills: Investment for reform.* London: Author.

Dicembre, E. (2002). How they turned the ship around. *Journal of Staff Development, 23*(2), 32–35.

Duke, D. (1988). Why principals consider quitting. *Phi Delta Kappan, 70*(4), 308–313.

Edge, K., Rolheiser, C., & Fullan, M. (2001). *Case studies of literacy driven educational change: The Toronto District School Board's early years literacy project.* Toronto, Ontario, Canada: University of Toronto, Ontario Institute for Studies in Education.

Edge, K., Rolheiser, C., & Fullan, M. (2002). *Case studies of assessment literacy-driven change: Edmonton Catholic Schools.* Toronto, Ontario, Canada: University of Toronto, Ontario Institute for Studies in Education.

Edu-Con. (1984). *The role of the public school principal in the Toronto Board of Education.* Toronto, Ontario, Canada: Author.

Elmore, R., & Burney, D. (1999). Investing in teacher learning. In L. Darling Hammond & G. Sykes (Eds.), *Teaching as the learning profession* (pp. 236–291). San Francisco: Jossey-Bass.

Evans, R. (1995, April 12). Getting real about leadership. *Education Week.*

Evans, R. (1996). *The human side of school change.* San Francisco: Jossey-Bass.

Fink, E., & Resnick, L. (2001). Developing principals as instructional leaders. *Phi Delta Kappan, 82,* 598–606.

Fullan, M. (1993). *Change forces: Probing the depths of educational reform.* London: Falmer.

Fullan, M. (1997). *What's worth fighting for in the principalship?* (2nd ed.). New York: Teachers College Press.

Fullan, M. (1999). *Change forces: The sequel.* London: Falmer.

Fullan, M. (2001a). *The new meaning of educational change* (3rd ed.). New York: Teachers College Press.

Fullan, M. (2001b). *Leading in a culture of change.* San Francisco: Jossey-Bass.

Fullan, M. (2003). *Change forces with a vengeance.* London: Falmer.

Gerstner, L., Jr. (2002). *Who says elephants can't dance. Inside IBM's historic turnaround.* New York: Harper Business.

Gladwell, M. (2000). *The tipping point.* Boston: Little, Brown.

Goodlad, J. (2002). Kudzu, rabbit, and school reform. *Phi Delta Kappan, 84*(1), 16–23.

Hargreaves, A. (in press). *Teaching in the knowledge society.* New York: Teachers College Press.

Heifetz, R., & Linsky, M. (2002). *Leadership on the line: Staying alive through the dangers of leading.* Boston: Harvard Business School Press.

Hess, F. (1999). *Spinning wheels. The politics of urban school reform.* Washington, DC: Brookings Institute.

Hesselbein, F. (2002). *Hesselbein on leadership.* San Francisco: Jossey-Bass.

Hilton, S., & Gibbons, G. (2002). *Good business.* London: TEXERE Publishing.

Kotter, J., & Cohen, D. (2002). *The heart of change.* Boston: Harvard Business School Press.

Leithwood, K., Fullan, M., & Watson, N. (2003). *The schools we need.* Toronto, Ontario, Canada: Atkinson Foundation.

Livsey, R., & Palmer, P. J. (1999). *The courage to teach: A guide to reflection and renewal.* San Francisco: Jossey-Bass.

Martin, R. (2002). *The responsibility virus.* New York. Basic Books.

Mascall, B., Fullan, M., & Rolheiser, C. (2001). *The challenges of coherence and capacity.* Toronto, Ontario, Canada: University of Toronto, Ontario Institute for Studies in Education.

Miliband, D. (2002a). *Speech. Annual Meeting of the Association for Foundation and Voluntary Aides Schools.* London: Department for Education and Skills.

Miliband, D. (2002b). *Speech. Conference of Independent/State School Partnerships.* Brighton, England: Author.

National College for School Leadership. (2002). *Prospectus.* Nottingham, England: Author.

Newmann, F., King, B., & Youngs, P. (2000, April). *Professional development that addresses school capacity.* Paper presented at the annual meeting of the American Educational Research Association, New Orleans.

Organization for Economic Cooperation and Development. (2000). *Knowledge and skills for life: First results from PISA 2000.* Paris: Author.

Patterson, J., Purkey, S., & Parker, J. (1986). *Productive school systems for a non-rational world.* Alexandria, VA: Association for Supervision and Curriculum Development.

Reina, D., & Reina, M. (1999). *Trust and betrayal in the workplace.* San Francisco: Berrett-Koehler.

Rolheiser, C., Fullan, M., & Edge, K. (in press). Literacy expertise is not enough: Developing literacy change agentry. *Journal of Staff Development, 24*(2).

Sarason, S. (1982). *The culture of the school and the problem of change* (2nd ed.). Boston: Allyn & Bacon.

Snipes, J., Doolittle, F., & Herlihy, C. (2002). *Foundations for success: Case studies of how urban school systems improve student achievement.* Washington, DC: Council of Great City Schools.

Spence, C. (2002). *On time! On task! On a mission!* Black Point, Nova Scotia: Fernwood.

Spillane, J., Diamond, J., Burch, P., Hallett, T., Jita, J., & Zoltners, J. (2002). Managing in the middle: School leaders and the enactment of accountability policy. *Educational Policy, 16*(5), 731–762.

Storr, A. (1988). *Solitude.* London: Flamingo Press.

Stringer, R. (2002). *Leadership and organizational climate.* Upper Saddle River, NJ: Prentice Hall.

Urdang, L. (1992). *The Oxford Thesaurus.* New York: Oxford University.

Williams, T. (2001). *Unrecognized exodus, unaccepted accountability: The looming shortage of principals and vice-principals in Ontario Public School Boards.* Toronto, Ontario, Canada: Ontario Principals' Council.

Index

**CORWIN
PRESS**

The Corwin Press logo—a raven striding across an open book—represents the happy union of courage and learning. We are a professional-level publisher of books and journals for K-12 educators, and we are committed to creating and providing resources that embody these qualities. Corwin's motto is "Success for All Learners."